JAMES BUCHANAN

JAMES BUCHANAN

by EDWIN P. HOYT

REILLY & LEE COMPANY · CHICAGO

TABLE OF CONTENTS

CHAPTER 1

The Formative Years,
1791–1820

AT THE MID-POINT of the nineteenth century, it
seemed that all the heat and hatred of the years was focused
in Washington, the capital of the United States of America.
The United States was just three-quarters of a century old
as a nation, but in the 1850's it seemed most unlikely that
she could survive much longer. It was apparent that the
warring colonies which had united against the callous
motherland in 1775 had very little in common. Stripped of
all the normal differences of a growing nation in a wilder-
ness continent, the economic and social differences of the
United States were vast: the country was split horizontally
by an old survey line called the Mason-Dixon line, which
ran along the Maryland-Pennsylvania border. South of that
line lay the states which honored the old practice of slavery;
north of that line slavery was abhorred and had been largely
outlawed for a quarter of a century.

At one time there had been slaves in the North. Men
from the South and from the West Indies had come to New
York and Boston and Philadelphia, bringing their Negro
slave servants with them. But in the colder, less productive
lands of the northern states slavery had never prospered.
Land holdings were small, for the most part, and the need
for a vast supply of intelligent labor was small. Before the

invention of the cotton gin, and the other revolutionary farm machinery which followed almost immediately, one could see the economic argument for slavery, or at least for the continuance of the use of cheap human labor on the vast estates of the South. But in the North, even had there been similar argument, slavery was bound to die out. The northern states were the haven of the growing middle class, and the workers of the lower middle class found themselves in competition with slaves. So slavery died out quickly enough, but only in the North; in the South it flourished and was protected by men who refused to look at the economic issue.

The issues were two: first, the moral issue of slavery, which mocked the high-flown words of the writers of the American Constitution and its amendments; second, the economic issue of slavery and of slave states and free states. Soon, because of the social structure in the South, the huge landholders dominated all the southern states, and they protected their own rights as they saw them. This domination prevented the growth of an industrial economy. In the North, where economic opportunity was greater and a man might rise quickly through his own inventiveness, the industrial system flourished. Thus, to the North flowed the capital needed for growth and business. By 1850, the North was the wealthy section of the country; the huge estates of the South masked the relative poverty of the whole region.

At this time there came to the Presidency of the United States a man who had grown up in public life, living with the growing conflict every day. James Buchanan had served his people and his country in every delicate position, as state legislator, congressman, diplomat, senator, and Secretary of State. The very state from which he came—Pennsylvania—was a bastion of anti-slavery sentiment, and yet there were people in the state, living on the borders in the farmlands, whose neighbors kept slaves in Maryland, across the Mason-Dixon line, and who could not see what the argument was all about. In a manner of speaking, the issue of slavery was as dominant in Pennsylvania as in Washington, for the nearness of slavery kept emotions high and the problems always before men of public spirit. James Buchanan, son of a farmer and merchant, had lived with the problem of slavery all of his life and had watched it grow to become a monster. He was symbolic of this time— he, who would sit in the presidential chair in the White House working all during his term of office to preserve the Union, and watch helplessly as men heedlessly plunged toward the bloody conflict that would stain the hearths of nearly every household in the nation with the blood of the young men.

James Buchanan was a second-generation American, born of parents who had similar backgrounds. Both his mother and his father were of Scotch-Irish descent, and they were Presbyterian and religious by nature. His father had come from County Donegal in Ireland when he was twenty-two years old, leaving Ireland just before the signing of the peace treaty between the new American nation and England. He went first to Philadelphia, and then to York County to stay with relatives. He made several moves in the next few years, trying to establish himself in business. Finally he settled at the Cove Gap, a place where western settlers came with their pack horses loaded with wheat and furs to trade for salt, metal implements, and farm goods. The elder Buchanan bought his manufactured goods from Baltimore and sold them to these westerners, building a thriving business in general merchandise. Soon he was prosperous enough to buy land.

In the spring of 1788, the elder Buchanan, also named James, married Elizabeth Speer, who came from a farm family that lived between Chambersburg and Gettysburg. Elizabeth was twenty-one and the elder James Buchanan was twenty-seven. Young James was born on April 23, 1791, the second of eleven children.

Five years after the boy's birth, in 1796, the Buchanan family moved to Mercersburg, where the elder Buchanan established a mercantile business and continued to farm outside the town. Young James grew up learning both the business of storekeeping and the arts of farming. His father was one of the most respected men in the area, and he served at various times as justice of peace. His mother, the daughter of a farmer and now wife of one, had very little opportunity for formal education. Late in the eighteenth century girls were taught to sew and to do needlework, to knit, and even to spin. They learned music if the family was prosperous enough to own a musical instrument. They learned to read and write, but more attention was paid to their learning to write a round, attractive hand and to answer social letters than to studying the classics or the courses necessary for a young man entering the professions. Elizabeth Buchanan grew up in a household where the girls were expected to help with the cooking, canning, housekeeping, and inside chores, and she spent much of her time mending and sewing. But she developed a fondness for poetry which was quite unusual in an uneducated girl, and she studied the poets. She read Milton's poetry, as well as his prose, and the works of Alexander Pope, William Cowper, and James Thomson, all well-known poets of the day. She took a lively interest in the church, which was proper for a young woman, and she led her children to become well-versed in religious matters.

The elder James Buchanan was opinionated in the matter of religion, as so many of the early Americans were, for religion in the early nineteenth century played a far more important role in the lives of ordinary men than it would a century later. The elder Buchanan quarreled with one minister and left his church forever. But he joined Elizabeth's Presbyterian group even before they were married, and he remained a Presbyterian for the rest of his life.

Young James was fortunate in that his parents could afford a better education for him than could most. He studied at a grammar school in Mercersburg and learned to read and write and to do simple arithmetic. Many boys learned this much; the difference came later when James received an excellent grounding in English, and then began the study of Latin and Greek. His first teacher was the Reverend James R. Sharon, a young divinity student who was earning his way in the world by taking students. Later, James studied under Jesse Magaw, a doctor who was well-versed in the classics.

In 1807 James Buchanan entered Dickinson College in Carlisle, Pennsylvania. He was only sixteen years old, but he was well enough along in his studies to be admitted to the junior class.

As James later wrote in his autobiographical notes, it was a serious mistake for him to be sent to Dickinson. There was little discipline at the college, and James Buchanan was a boy of lively interests. He managed, from the beginning, to be in trouble with the school authorities for his capers. His one saving grace, apparently, was aptitude for hard study as well as for merry-making, because he achieved high marks in his courses, even though he was usually in disgrace with his masters.

At the end of his first year at Dickinson College, James returned home on vacation during September. One Sunday morning when he was sitting in the parlor with his father, a letter was brought for the elder Buchanan. It came from the college.

As the letter was opened James waited with interest. His father read the letter, his face assuming a pained expression as he read. When the elder Buchanan finished, he handed the letter to James and left the room without a word.

James looked down at the paper. The letter came from Dr. Davidson, the principal of the college. He began at the beginning and read.

Had the officers and members of the faculty not held the elder Buchanan in such respect, said Dr. Davidson, young James would have been expelled during the school year for disorderly conduct. They had tolerated his improprieties out of that respect, but the college would not take him back for a second year.

James did not discuss the letter with his father, then or ever again. That day he went to the rectory of the Presbyterian church to call on Dr. John King, pastor and one of the well-known Presbyterian theologians of the time. Dr. King had a high reputation throughout Pennsylvania. Even more important to James, he was a trustee of Dickinson College.

James Buchanan explained his predicament. Dr. King was a fair and just man, and he had the highest respect for the Buchanan family. He proposed that if James would pledge his honor to behave properly while at Carlisle, he, in turn, would intercede and take the responsibility for the young Buchanan's behavior while at the college. James returned then to Dickinson College for his senior year, and no more complaints were heard about his conduct.

Yet James could not remain out of trouble. When it came time for him to graduate, he sailed through the oral examinations which professors then conducted to assure themselves that the young men were capable of receiving their degrees without bringing disrepute on the college. He did not fail to answer a single question correctly. All year long, James had shown his academic superiority, and was a favorite among the students, besides. He was a member of a literary society at the college and his society nominated him for honors. Another literary society existed at Dickinson College then, and it was the custom for the faculty to confer two special honors, one on the candidate of each society.

James set his heart on winning the highest honor, but that was not all. During the year, his society had so far outstripped the other in matters of scholarship, that he led the others in a move to secure both honors for his society. This was unprecedented, and when the word leaked out the professors were annoyed.

When the time came for decision, three candidates had been nominated for the two honors. The professors ignored James Buchanan and awarded the honors to the other two men. They explained that they had excluded James because it would be unseemly to confer an honor on a student who had so little respect for the traditions of the college and so little liking for the faculty that he had posed this problem to them.

The students rose up in protest. In James's society, Robert Laverty, who had received the honor James sought, offered to give it to James. James declined. The other members of the society said they would all refuse to appear at the commencement exercises. James liked this idea, but since several members of his class were heading for the ministry, and it would not do for them to be involved in controversy, he persuaded the others not to make a public demonstration. He decided that he, alone, would refuse to attend the commencement exercises, where he was to speak. Eventually, however, he changed his mind, for several members of the faculty wrote to him saying that they held kindly feelings toward him. He attended the commencement exercises, but left college without any friendly feelings for his old school. He would never have them.

At the time of this struggle in the summer of 1809, James wrote home to report about it to his father and mother. His father replied at some length, in a letter remarkable for its worldliness and understanding.

The family was disappointed, his father wrote, particularly since the professors were "acknowledged by the world to be the best judges of the talents and merits" of the students. It would have been far better, said the elder Buchanan, if James had accepted the situation as it existed and tried only for the one honor for himself instead of attempting to change the system.

"The more you know of mankind," said the elder Buchanan, "the more you will distrust them. It is said that the knowledge of mankind and the distrust of them are reciprocally connected. . . ."

Those were harsh words, and they had their effect on James, coming as they did at the height of a serious disappointment. Nonetheless, they were good training for a young man who hoped, as James now did, to become a student and practitioner of the law. He was only eighteen years old, and had suffered his first serious disappointment, yet he had emerged with honor in the eyes of his equals.

In September, after graduation, James went home for a brief vacation. He spent much of the next two months tramping through the nearby woods, carrying a squirrel rifle and bringing home the ingredients for squirrel stew, one of his favorite dishes. He was a good shot and a good athlete —young, slender, and strong. He soon forgot the smart of the events of the summer, but not the lesson. By December James was ready to push ahead in seeking his career. He traveled that month to Lancaster, Pennsylvania, where he would begin the study of the law as a clerk in the office of James Hopkins.

James embarked on his studies with vigor and purpose; he was determined to understand every part of the law. He worked and studied during the days, and in the evenings he took long walks in the woods, practicing speeches in which he put into his own words what he had learned. Thus, he became a lawyer who understood the law and, of more importance to his future, a speaker who knew how to use words and to create convincing arguments.

He was tempted still by the easy life of the taverns in Lancaster, but he discussed this problem openly with his father in letters and was warned against self-indulgence.

James studied for three years in the Hopkins office before he and his employer, who was also his sponsor, agreed that he was ready to seek admission to the bar. He was accepted as a practicing lawyer in November, 1812, a few months after the United States and Britain went to war for the second time.

During the first two years of the war against Britain, James Buchanan argued against the war, as did most of the members of the Federalist movement, to which he adhered. But in the summer of 1814, when the British burned Washington and threatened Baltimore, even those who had opposed the war as costly and useless were stirred to protest. Buchanan made his first public speech at a public meeting in Lancaster, which was called to raise volunteers to march toward Baltimore and forestall the British under General Robert Ross. Buchanan rushed to the podium, put his name down as one of the first to volunteer, and harangued his fellow townsmen about the need for unity and strength to conquer the invaders. Within a matter of hours this force elected a captain and decided that the men would serve as *dragoons,* that is, as soldiers on horseback who also carried short muskets so that they were able to fight as either infantry or as cavalry.

The Pennsylvania dragoon company of Lancaster marched off to Baltimore, where it served for several weeks under Major Charles Sterret Ridgely. When the British threat was gone, the dragoons were discharged and sent back to their homes and businesses.

So, James Buchanan had, in the service of his country, tasted public life of a sort, and he found it most agreeable.

As a lawyer he depended for his business on word of mouth and his own notoriety. In the first year of his law practice, 1813, he earned only a little more than $900; in his second year, he earned a hundred dollars more. Searching for a way to increase his income, he decided to run for the state house of representatives as a legislator from Lancaster County.

In the legislature, in 1815, Representative Buchanan made his maiden speech on the subject of conscription. It was the burning issue of the moment, and with good reason. The British were threatening Philadelphia, and the state government, close to bankruptcy, could not raise a force of paid soldiers to protect the city, at least not a force of mercenaries. The federal government was in worse straits in matters of manpower and money because of the unpopularity of the war and because of the evasions of the states in meeting their obligations for the common good.

Two plans were put forward by the members of the Pennsylvania legislature to raise a force that would defend the commonwealth, one of which called for conscription. Under this measure all the men in the state would be divided into groups of twenty-two men each. Every man between the ages of eighteen and forty-five would be subject to conscription. The conscript from each group would be chosen by lot, and after the one man was chosen, the other twenty-one in his group would have to raise $200 which the chosen man would receive as his bounty. He would serve one year and then be free, while another man was chosen and the bounty subscribed again. The army would be paid by the state.

The second plan was offered: to raise six regiments of militia to serve for three years, as volunteers. There now seems to be relatively little difference between the two plans, but a hundred and fifty years after the discussions took place in the Pennsylvania legislature it is difficult to reconstruct the emotions and logic of that day. Representative Buchanan arose in the state house of representatives to state his position, with considerable heat.

First, he took note of the "desertion" of the people of Pennsylvania by the federal Congress, speaking with the bitterness of a Federalist who had opposed the war in the first place and was indignant because the federal government had refused to prosecute that war without imposing on the treasuries of the states.

But more important, Buchanan said, was the impropriety of the conscription bill. Most of the valuable property of Pennsylvania was located in the older, more inhabited eastern half of the state. Western Pennsylvania was, in 1815, frontier territory, settled in small plots by poor farmers who had traveled west seeking opportunity. There was very little money in the western section of the state. Yet, the twenty-two men in the western area would be required to raise the same sum as twenty-two men in Philadelphia, although the combined wealth of the westerners might be $2,000 and that of the Philadelphians might be $2,000,000. And what was to be defended? Philadelphia, in particular.

The issue was debated with much heat in the Pennsylvania legislature. The senate passed the conscription bill, but it was defeated in the house, which passed the volunteer bill. Before a compromise or a deadlock could be said to exist, the war ended, and the issue was dropped.

As far as James Buchanan was concerned, the importance of the military issue lay in its effect on his reputation and career. One of the leading figures in the Pennsylvania party of Jeffersonian Democratic Republicans (later to become the Democratic party) came to him, suggesting that he change his party affiliation from Federalist. In the state house of representatives, said this Jeffersonian, Representative Buchanan had been talking like a fellow Democrat. Why did he not join the party? Buchanan refused. He said he was not willing even to consider such a course.

After the signing of the Treaty of Ghent, which ended the War of 1812, James Buchanan was undecided as to what course he ought to pursue. He wrote to his father, in doubt as to whether or not he should again seek a seat in the state legislature.

The elder Buchanan was a practical man. In his reply he noted that young James had not suffered by his experience in the legislature; indeed, as James had claimed, the associations in the state capital had brought him new business, and in 1815 he would earn more than $2,000. So there was no objection to his returning to the legislature, in fact, it might even be helpful. His father also suggested that if James wanted to remain in public life he ought to seek election to Congress.

In the summer of 1815 James practiced law and engaged in political campaigning around the countryside of Lancaster. That year, he gave the Independence Day oration before the Washington Association of Lancaster, and men, women, and children from the rural community trooped into town to sit on the green beneath the platform and listen to the band and the speaker. James was young and filled with idealism. He traced the story of the recent war, blaming the Madison administration and the hotheads in Congress for starting the war, and criticizing Congress for its conduct of the war. For the heroism of the navy, however, he had nothing but praise.

James Buchanan's oration was long and fiery, in the tradition of the day. However, he learned much from it. For one thing, he learned the importance of moderation. Because he had criticized Congress for its activities, he lost old friends who leaned to the Democratic cause.

In September, James decided that he would run again for the legislature, and he began campaigning in earnest, giving up a vacation with his family to do so. The election was held in October, and he was again chosen to represent the people of Lancaster in the state house of representatives.

James returned to the legislature in the autumn of 1815 to face one of the most important political issues of the day, an issue that would dominate American domestic politics for a quarter of a century: the problem of banking and currency control.

As with any young nation, the United States was established with little money and very little credit with other nations. Paper money was first issued during the Revolutionary War, and some of it was never redeemed by the government. (The saying "not worth a continental" referred to the Continental Congress paper money that was worthless at the end of the Revolution.) Then, disastrously soon after the Revolutionary War, came the War of 1812, which forced the federal government to build an expensive navy. This war also brought about a blockade and the suspension of trade with European nations for nearly four years. At the end of the war, American business had many serious problems. One of them concerned the great amount of paper money that had been issued again to pay for the war.

This money was issued by various banks, whose activities were controlled by the states. Thus there were different laws concerning the issuing of money in all the states.

Foreign countries and foreign businessmen did not have any faith in the paper money issued by these local banks, and they insisted on being paid for goods and debts in gold and silver. So the supply of gold and silver grew very short in the United States, and, in the autumn of 1815, men and women who went to their banks with paper money discovered that they often could not get gold or silver for these paper notes, which were really nothing more than bank promises to pay in gold or silver. It would be going too far to say that public confidence was shattered, but it was seriously strained. In 1815, men and women in America much preferred to be paid in coins or goods. Paper money was regarded as a nuisance, and sometimes as a fraud.

James Buchanan went to the legislature that year to consider ways to remedy the banking situation. The Pennsylvania legislature studied the laws, and a committee recommended that banks be given a year in which to redeem their paper money. During that year, they would have to pay the holders of the paper money six percent interest. At the end of the year they would have to pay eighteen percent interest per year if they did not redeem the paper currency. If they did not pay the notes off by January 1, 1818, they would be forced out of business.

That was the report of the majority of a committee in the legislature. But James prepared a minority report which recommended that no compulsory measure be taken regarding banking. The result was a long argument which was never settled. James Buchanan became an ardent opponent of the idea of a United States bank, a central bank that would take care of government funds and would issue currency. Like the other opponents of the central bank, he was against putting so much power into a few hands. Such a bank had been the central part of Alexander Hamilton's plan for the financing of the infant United States government. The charter of the first-Bank of the United States had expired just before the outbreak of the War of 1812 and it was never renewed. That, said the proponents of the national bank, was the main reason for the difficulty in supporting the War of 1812. A second bank was chartered in 1816 after a harsh debate in Congress in which many men crossed party lines to vote as their consciences directed them. James Buchanan sided with the views of President Madison and Daniel Webster, who opposed the bank although of course the young Pennsylvania legislator was unknown to these powerful political figures, while John C. Calhoun and Henry Clay favored the bank as necessary to restore sound currency to the United States.

After the legislative session of 1816, James Buchanan decided that politics had nothing to offer him. His father approved of this decision. He believed that his son should devote himself to the making of his fortune. James began to devote his full time to his law practice, and in the next three years he tripled his income, earning in 1818 and 1819 more than $7,000 annually.

During the next session of the legislature, an attempt was made to impeach a Pennsylvania judge for a decision he had made regarding the powers of the state government as opposed to the powers of the federal government. (The judge had held that when a militiaman was called into federal service the state had no further power over him. It was a most unpopular decision.) James's defense of the judge was strong and spirited and it brought him a greater reputation than his service in the legislature had. The next year there were similar cases, and he was called upon to defend other officials against impeachment, and again he handled himself well.

In 1819 James Buchanan was twenty-eight years old and

his income was such that he could be regarded as one of the most eligible bachelors of the community. That year he was courting a young woman, Anne Coleman, and they became engaged. Then, in the summer, James was involved in an indiscretion of the sort that had caused him so much trouble during his college years. At least Anne Coleman regarded his action as indiscreet, and she broke off the engagement. Her father, who had wholeheartedly approved of James as a prospective son-in-law, forbade him the house. James wrote letters, but they were returned unopened.

In December, Anne Coleman went to visit friends in Philadelphia, and, while there, she fell ill and died. James wrote to Robert Coleman, asking that he be allowed to see his beloved's body before she was buried and to join the mourners. His letter was returned unopened.

The tragedy was very real for James. He fled Lancaster, telling no one where he was going, and he remained away from his law practice for several weeks. Then, when he returned to Lancaster he found his world empty. He had given up politics, bent on earning money and marrying and raising a family. Suddenly money meant nothing to him, and he was eager to be away from Lancaster. A friend suggested that if James wished he could have the nomination of the Federalists for Congress from that district. His life had changed so much, so quickly, that James decided this was exactly what he wanted to do. So in the spring of 1820 he allowed his name to be put up for the nomination. He won it and then began to campaign for election in the counties of Lancaster, York, and Dauphin. He was elected to the House of Representatives in the fall of that year and went to Washington.

CHAPTER 2

Congressman

THE SEVENTEENTH CONGRESS of the United States convened on December 3, 1821, just after the Missouri Compromise brought that state into the Union as a slave state. Hopes were high in Washington that Speaker of the House Henry Clay had achieved the impossible—had quieted the disagreement between North and South on the issue of slavery.

However, with Missouri's admission to the Union came the first outspoken attempts of the growing number of abolitionists in the North to put an end to slavery. The Missouri Compromise had been achieved largely through the negotiating genius of Clay, and for a short time it appeared that the difficulties between slave states and free states had been resolved. Maine came into the Union as a free state. Those parts of the Louisiana Purchase territory which lay north of 36°30′ were declared to be out of bounds for slavery, which meant that when states were finally organized in the territory they would be free states. These agreements seemed to pacify the abolitionists. The territory south of 36°30′ was not restricted. The chess game of trading—a slave state to be admitted for every free state—was begun, and this haphazard approach to the schism between two social systems was to continue for forty years.

Beneath the surface the seeds of the Civil War were growing strong, but on the surface there was no period in American history in which there seemed to be so great a degree of unanimity of political viewpoint. This period was known as the Era of Good Feeling. Two years earlier, between May and September, President Monroe had toured the eastern part of America and had traveled west as far as Detroit. He had been greeted with cheers nearly everywhere, even by men in New England who might have been considered to be his political enemies.

The sharp lines that separated the Federalists and the Democratic Republicans had disappeared with the end of the War of 1812. A political opposition existed—the Missouri Compromise was passed by a vote of 134-42 in the House of Representatives—but the opposition was not nearly so well organized as it had been in earlier times, and the issues that divided men were not easily seen in the political measures before Congress.

The cabinet was composed of men of various political beliefs, who came from all sections of the country. In the North, most people advocated free trade because it was beneficial to northern manufacturing and agriculture. In the middle states, many wanted moderate protection of industries, because this would improve their competitive position in those particular industries for which there was competition from abroad. The South, which sold its cotton abroad, wanted only a few items regulated by the tariff.

Aside from the issue of the tariff, a major difference of viewpoint was emerging in the attitudes toward federal financing of various government projects, such as roads and canals. Those who would be directly helped by such projects favored them. Others believed that the states in which the improvements were planned should pay for them.

In the House, James Buchanan's political philosophy was

forged, issue by issue. A bankruptcy bill was brought before the House. It related almost entirely to commercial firms, because the idea of protecting the middle-class or lower-class individual against payment of excessive debt had not been raised as a federal question. (Debtors were covered by state laws.) This legislation was aimed to cover large firms, such as banks, that dealt in interstate commerce.

One member of the House suggested that the measure should cover all cases of insolvency. Buchanan objected. He raised the moral issue of a wealthy citizen who goes bankrupt, becomes affluent again, and refuses to pay his old debts. He raised the question of states' responsibilities and rights versus federal, and said that the law would bring about "judicial consolidation" of the Union, which he opposed. The Union was an association of independent commonwealths, each designed to govern itself in internal matters, and he did not wish to see the symmetry of this system disturbed.

Another issue on which James Buchanan took a stand was that of the Cumberland Road. Before Buchanan entered Congress, the federal government had built a public road which extended from Cumberland, Maryland, to Wheeling, Virginia. (Wheeling is now part of West Virginia.) This road crossed Maryland, passed through Pennsylvania, and then cut across part of Virginia. Pennsylvanians, in particular, did not like the Cumberland Road because a group of Pennsylvania businessmen had built a toll road between Philadelphia and Pittsburgh, at private expense, for private profit. The federal road, which was free for travelers, was in competition with the toll road, and its owners opposed government competition with free enterprise.

In the congressional session of 1822, the Cumberland Road question came before the House when an attempt was made to appropriate money for repair of the road. The opponents of the highway chose this measure to show their dislike of the entire project. Buchanan voted with others to impose tolls on the Cumberland Road to pay for the repairs, rather than to take the money out of the general funds. His position was based on a belief in the competitive idea.

However, this measure brought up the entire question of federal and state powers, when President Monroe vetoed the bill on principle. Congress did not have the power to impose tolls, he said, nor did the states of the nation have the right to grant further powers to Congress by directing the votes of their members of Congress. Congress had only the power to tax for the general good.

During the next session of Congress, Buchanan took the position that the federal government should not be involved in the road project, since it was of benefit to only three states. He moved to have the Cumberland Road turned over to the three states through which it passed, but the move was rejected. Buchanan also took a position in favor of a high tariff, because this was in the interest of Pennsylvania manufacturers and farmers.

In the autumn of 1824, Representative Buchanan became personally involved in an unpleasant controversy between Senator Andrew Jackson and Secretary of State John Quincy Adams. Buchanan knew both men, but not well. He also knew Henry Clay, who was Speaker of the House in 1824.

Jackson and Adams competed in the race for the Presidency, and, when neither secured a majority of electoral votes, the matter was taken before the House of Representatives. Then came what Andrew Jackson always regarded bitterly as a "political deal" between Adams and Henry Clay, in which Clay traded his support in the House for the promise that he would be appointed Secretary of State. At that time, the political tradition of the new nation indicated that the Secretary of State would be the next President.

Clay had also been running for the Presidency; however, it was apparent in the election returns that he was not to have it, so he set out to strengthen his position as best he could.

At that time various pressures were brought to bear on members of the House to vote for one man or the other. Clay's friends were trying to secure promises from both candidates that they would appoint Clay Secretary of State, and thus heir-apparent to the Presidency. The rumor arose that if Andrew Jackson was elected he would continue John Quincy Adams in the State Department post. James Buchanan had been a warm supporter of Jackson in the campaign, although he also was friendly to Clay. He was not friendly, nor were many of his constituents, to John Quincy Adams; largely in the tariff matter the middle states moved away from the New Englander.

Several of Buchanan's friends asked him to see General Jackson in order to find out where the General stood on the matter of Secretary of State. One, Representative Philip Markley of Pennsylvania, a Clay supporter, asked Buchanan to try to persuade "Old Hickory" to come out for Clay for Secretary of State or to refuse to take a position between Clay and Adams. Either way, Clay's position would be strengthened.

James Buchanan called on Andrew Jackson at his lodgings and walked with the General to the War Department, where the Tennesseean had business to conduct for his constituents. They talked politics. Buchanan asked bluntly if the General proposed to keep John Quincy Adams in his cabinet and, particularly, if he had promised to do so, as the rumors claimed. General Jackson said he had made no such promise. He liked Adams well enough, he said, but he had made no commitments one way or another.

Buchanan mentioned the remarks of his fellow congressman from Pennsylvania, Mr. Markley, who wanted Clay appointed if Jackson was elected. Nothing more was said.

Then came the election in the House and the disappointment of General Jackson, the election of Adams, and the appointment of Henry Clay as Secretary of State.

During the months that followed, General Jackson recognized James Buchanan as one of his best supporters in Pennsylvania, and their correspondence in 1825 and 1826 was warm and frequent. But in 1827, someone persuaded Jackson that Buchanan had been trying to make "a deal" for Clay, just as other politicians seemed to have made a deal for Clay with Adams. Jackson became angry and made several rash statements to the press, which severely injured Buchanan's position. On July 15, from the Hermitage, Jackson wrote a cold note to Buchanan asking him to come forth with "the facts." Buchanan then had his story published in the Lancaster *Journal*. It was circulated widely, and was later published in other newspapers. The tempest continued for some months, but died down after Jackson's election in 1828.

Buchanan was upset by Jackson's readiness to believe evil of him, because he was one of the General's most earnest supporters in Congress. In 1825 and 1826, along with Representative James Knox Polk of Tennessee, Buchanan was one of the opposition members who combined to make the Adams administration wretched. When President Adams proposed to send ministers to a hemispheric conference in Panama, Congress balked and sneered and delayed the program until it was too late. James Buchanan took a part in the resistance; he favored appropriating the money to send the emissaries, but he proposed that Congress should dictate the emissaries' actions in Panama. In speaking on this issue, James Buchanan stated his position on the question of slavery, a position that would become very important to the nation in the years ahead.

He did not like to talk about slavery, he said, and he hoped he would never have to speak on the subject again.

I believe it to be a great political and a great moral evil. I thank God my lot has been cast in a state where it does not exist. But, while I entertain these opinions, I know it is an evil at present without a remedy . . . one of those moral evils impossible for us to escape, without the introduction of evils infinitely greater. There are portions of this Union, in which, if you emancipate your slaves, they will become masters. There can be no middle course. Is there any man in this Union who could, for a moment, indulge in the horrible idea of abolishing slavery by the massacre of the high-minded and the chivalrous race of men in the South? I trust there is not one.

This interjection had little to do with the question of sending ambassadors to Panama, but much to do with the future of the nation.

For the next three years, Buchanan proved himself to be a good friend of General Jackson and an opponent of the theory of strong federal power advocated by John Quincy Adams. In 1828 he supported Jackson in spite of the unfortunate interpretation the old soldier had placed on his remarks on the Washington street that day in 1825. Buchanan sought no office for himself except reelection to Congress, which he obtained. He returned to Washington in the first session of the Twenty-first Congress in 1829, and was elected chairman of the judiciary committee of the House.

Now came a great change in politics and the political fortunes of James Buchanan. In 1829, Martin Van Buren resigned as governor of New York State to come to Washington as Secretary of State in the cabinet of Andrew Jackson, who had been elected easily enough. Immediately, Van Buren began to build the Democratic party by the use of patronage.

One of the direct recipients of Van Buren's patronage was James Buchanan. In November, 1830, his brother George was appointed district attorney for the Pittsburgh region. The letter came, interestingly enough, from Martin Van Buren, Secretary of State, enclosing the commission from Andrew Jackson, President of the United States. Van Buren was not one to allow patronage to rest in the hands of the Attorney-General in this case.

Presentation to a Buchanan of this political plum was a sure indication that the breach between Buchanan and Jackson was healed, for although Van Buren exercised great power in the Jackson administration, he would not have appointed a Jackson enemy to office.

The judiciary committee concerned itself with the building of the American judicial system and the reform of some of the aspects of American justice. Buchanan managed the impeachment of a federal judge from Missouri, who was accused of having misused his authority in a personal feud, and, although the impeachment was narrowly defeated, the principle of judicial responsibility was strengthened.

Buchanan decided, sometime in 1830, that he would retire from public life and return to full practice at the bar. The personal disappointments of his life had passed, and he could bear to go home again to Pennsylvania to live. His income from the law had dropped from nearly $11,000 a year to about $2,000 a year, and he felt that he must rebuild his practice.

Early in 1831 some of Buchanan's friends decided they would put him up for the Vice-Presidency, as part of the

Jackson ticket in the election of 1832. There was considerable agitation in Pennsylvania, particularly among the enemies of Martin Van Buren, but it came to very little. Buchanan did retire from Congress; he did not seek re-election, and his last day in the House was spent on March 3, 1831. He was not insensitive to the demand that he become a candidate for the Vice-Presidency, but he had no desire to alienate Van Buren, and when friends wrote him about the prospect he replied that he had no ambitions. It was a typical, careful reply. He did not forbid his friends to seek the post for him, but in his disregard for it he disarmed his potential political enemies.

In spite of a number of efforts to nominate Buchanan along with Jackson in the state of Pennsylvania, the movement did not come to much. Buchanan's name was mentioned prominently in the newspapers in the spring of 1831, and there was much attention in his favor at various Democratic political gatherings throughout the nation.

Secretary of State Van Buren was not unmindful of the power Buchanan exerted in Pennsylvania, and, for a number of reasons, Van Buren was not popular in Pennsylvania. It was not surprising, then, that in the spring, as the movement for Buchanan gained strength, Buchanan was offered an important and interesting diplomatic post, that of Minister to Russia. The offer came indirectly, from John H. Eaton, a member of the "kitchen cabinet," which effectively directed the affairs of the White House for President Jackson. The offer was made secretly on May 31.

Buchanan was of two minds about accepting the appointment. He had no desire to quarrel with Van Buren, but he was seriously concerned about his law practice. He had returned to the practice of law with the vigor of a man who really meant what he said when he argued that he was going to remain in private life, and he had undertaken a number of commitments that would occupy him for several months.

Buchanan wrote to Eaton that he was flattered but that he was worried because of the language difficulty (Buchanan did not speak French, the official language of the Russian court) and because he had so many commitments. Eaton took up the matter with the President, who promised that Buchanan need not leave for Russia before the following winter or spring, as long as he arrived with the breaking of the ice for the season of 1832.

Buchanan then accepted. Privately he worried because the newspapers had already begun to speculate on his future, and some of them hinted that he was going to become Minister to Russia. Having accepted, he wished to begin studying French and to make arrangements to leave the country for a long period. He knew his action would tend to confirm the rumors, and so he asked President Jackson what he should do. Jackson replied that the gossip would not make any difference as long as Buchanan, himself, did not make any comments on the appointment at that time. The reason for this secrecy was that the office of Minister to Russia was then held by John Randolph of Virginia. Although Randolph's health was such that he could not spend very much time in the cold climate of Russia, and he wished to retire from the post, it would be most unseemly for a new appointment to be announced until Randolph did retire and return to the United States.

During the summer of 1931 James Buchanan was the subject of great political interest. He had decided against offering himself for the Vice-Presidency, and he so told Jackson in a letter, but the rumors continued. Also the rumors about his diplomatic appointment continued, and to confuse matters it still could not be announced. Then, Van Buren resigned as Secretary of State to become Minister to England, and this opened more political speculation. In the councils of the Democratic party, there was much argument about the direction in which the party should move. Some wanted the nomination of a vice-presidential candidate by the party, of a man who was pledged to be loyal to the party and the candidate. This was a reaction to the conduct of Vice-President John C. Calhoun, who had been elected in 1828, following the old system of running almost as an independent, with the hope that he might become President.

The system, as it existed, placed a premium on regional and state power within the political parties. Some, Van Buren among them, wanted party control of candidates to be exercised through the national convention, and the argument centered on this issue.

By the end of the year, Buchanan's appointment to the mission was made public, and the Senate confirmed the appointment without delay. Edward Livingston, the new Secretary of State, expressed his satisfaction in January and then began pressing Buchanan to leave for St. Petersburg. A new adventure was about to begin.

CHAPTER 3

Ambassador

JAMES BUCHANAN'S MOTHER was the only person who seemed to object to her son's proposed mission to Russia, and her objection was based on her advanced age and her conviction that she would not live to see her son again. She tried to persuade him not to make the trip, but he was committed, and he was looking forward to the adventure. Not so many Americans had been to Russia by 1832 that it could be regarded as anything else.

Buchanan's feelings alternated, however. Sometimes he felt exalted. Sometimes he was gloomy, particularly when he thought he would, as he described it, "leave the most free and happy country on earth for a despotism more severe than any which exists in Europe."

In March, James Buchanan left Lancaster by coach early one morning and arrived in Baltimore that same evening. The next day he went to Washington. There he received his passport and his instructions at the Department of State, called at the White House, and visited old friends.

One Sunday in April James Buchanan boarded the sailing ship "Silas Richards" in the harbor at New York, and the ship sailed that day for Liverpool, England. He was accompanied by Lieutenant John W. Barry of the United States Army, who was to serve as his private secretary, and by a

"mulatto servant" named Edward Landrick, who was apparently not a slave.

Middle age is not the best time for a man to begin to
learn something of the sea, and the forty-one year old Minister to Russia was seasick during most of the voyage. The
other passengers were ladies and gentlemen from both sides
of the Atlantic, and in the informal atmosphere they came
to know one another quite well.

The voyage between landfalls was short, as sailing voy-
ages went; they sailed on April 8, and on April 22 the "Silas
Richards" sighted Cape Clear, the southwestern point of the
Irish coast.

Buchanan and several other passengers decided they
would not wait longer, but would board a fishing boat and
go to Cork, and then on to Dublin. They packed up their
belongings, but the wind blew up and the sea became too
rough for an approach to the coast, so they, like the others,
were forced to wait until they reached Liverpool. The ship
came into that port at noon on May 3, after twenty-five days
at sea. Buchanan and his friends were lucky, in fact, that
they had been unable to land in Ireland because a cholera
epidemic had struck there, and many cases had been reported both in Cork and in Dublin. There was no cholera
in Liverpool.

So grateful were the passengers for their safe voyage that
they gave a dinner that night at the Adelphi Hotel in Liverpool, in honor of Captain Henry Holdridge. The American
consul came, but Minister Buchanan presided at the dinner, which was marked by many toasts, most of them to the
brave captain who had just completed his eighty-ninth safe
crossing of the Atlantic.

The next day Buchanan joined Mr. William Brown of
Liverpool for a tour of the sights. He found the people of
Liverpool very much like those of New York, and he was

handsomely entertained by the American consul and a large number of Englishmen.

From Liverpool, Buchanan traveled to Manchester by train, and then to London, stopping to visit such famous spots as Shakespeare's birthplace at Stratford-on-Avon, and Oxford, the university town. This sight-seeing was part of the tour that was expected of every American who went abroad. Buchanan visited cathedrals and other points of interest, but, as a politician, he was also interested in the people and their government. He found both decidedly inferior to the Americans and the American system. He wrote home to his brother Edward from London: ". . . I thank my God that I was born an American rather than an Englishman."

England was in turmoil, he reported. King William IV was extremely unpopular at the moment that Buchanan arrived in London, because he had refused to create a number of new peers in spite of strong public demand for more representative government. Buchanan's brother Edward was in the ministry, and so Buchanan discussed the state of the Church in England in his letter. He said it was not popular because tithing was still practiced, and many objected to paying by force a percentage of their income to the Church. Buchanan wrote, "The Church is not popular. Its rich livings are conferred upon the younger branches of noble houses." He disapproved of the class system and said he much preferred the American system under which ministers chose the ministry for reasons of conscience, and people provided for the ministers voluntarily.

Buchanan spent a few busy days in London. He attended the theater at Covent Garden and visited with the Russian ambassador, Prince Lieven. On May 18, he left England aboard the steamship that ran regularly to Hamburg. There were more entertainments in Hamburg and several sight-seeing expeditions around Germany and nearby points in Denmark. Then it was time to take the ship for Russia and his post at St. Petersburg.

It was June when Buchanan finally arrived in St. Petersburg, but the weather was very cold and the sky so bright at this time of year that at midnight he could read a newspaper in the street without a candle. In fact, he used no candles in his household during this season.

The weather was one objection that Americans found to Russia. They were not used to wearing cloaks in June. But an even greater objection was to the absence of political freedom. Buchanan wrote home to President Jackson on this subject: ". . . here there is no freedom of the press, no public opinion, and but little political conversation and that much guarded. In short, we live in the calm of despotism."

Buchanan was presented at court. Czar Nicholas I had little to say except to make small talk, but the Czarina had much to say, especially about the problem of the southern states in America. She had read of the inclination of some of the southern states to threaten to dissolve the Union, and she believed what she read. She insisted on discussing the social problems of America with Buchanan, much to his distaste. He told President Jackson that Europeans, even the Russians, believed that the severe conflicts of opinion in the United States between the North and South meant that a revolution would occur. Buchanan scoffed at this, but not wholeheartedly. "God forbid that the Union should be in any danger," he wrote.

Buchanan moved into a large, pleasant house on the Neva River, overlooking the harbor and the river traffic. Within a month, he concluded that, although Russia was despotic and there was absolutely no middle class, the serfs "are wholly unfit to take any share in the government, and it is doubtless the policy of the Emperor and nobles to keep them in this state of ignorance."

Buchanan's household included Lieutenant Barry and J. Randolph Clay, secretary of the legation. There was little to do except to keep up with the formalities of the Russian court, the most formal in Europe. Buchanan found that he was expected to drive a coach and four horses, with a servant behind who wore a special diplomatic uniform.

Just before the ice closed in for the winter, in November, Buchanan wrote to the President. He had made certain proposals about treaties to Count Nesselrode, the foreign minister, but nothing had yet come of them, he said. He also complained about the low salary and expense level allowed for the post at this expensive court. The American minister's salary came to only about $8,000 when it was changed into rubles. Even the king of Sardinia allowed his ambassador $16,000 a year for expenses, and the embassies of France and England gave their ambassadors far more money.

Buchanan had been sent to Russia with a definite purpose: to negotiate two treaties with the Russian government. One was to be a commercial treaty and the other was to safeguard American maritime rights in Russian territory.

In the matter of the first treaty, there were serious problems to be overcome. Count Nesselrode had not given much thought to relations with the United States because he was busy with affairs that involved the important powers in the world—France and England. But he was well-disposed to Buchanan, to whom he took an instant personal liking, and he was willing to listen to the American's arguments.

The problem did not lie with Count Nesselrode but with the Minister of Finance, Count Cancrene, a conservative of the old school who did not favor any special commercial treaties; with Baron Krudener, the Russian Minister to the United States, who had very little respect for America; and with Minister of the Interior Blondorff.

Early in October, Count Nesselrode called Buchanan to his office and reported that he had broached the matter of treaties with America but that the Emperor had refused to approve them. During the conversation he let the American minister know that this did not represent his viewpoint, but that the Emperor had been influenced by those in opposition. He suggested that before Buchanan report unfavorably to his government he submit the ideas again, making new arguments, especially about the importance of trade with the United States through the Black Sea, which had not been mentioned in detail. Count Nesselrode hoped to be able to convince the Czar that the treaties would be valuable to Russia.

It was unusual for a foreign minister to be so frank with a foreign diplomat as Count Nesselrode was with Buchanan, but it was due to Nesselrode's personal fondness for Buchanan, and the fact that the United States was so small a power and so inconsiderable as far as Russia was concerned that it was almost as if the two nations existed on separate planes.

Buchanan also was in the position of being a pawn in a private struggle for power in the Russian cabinet between Nesselrode and Count Cancrene.

After his long, friendly talk with Count Nesselrode, Buchanan went back to his legation and prepared the letter the Count had requested. He sent it to the foreign minister that very day. Time was important because the last ship out of the harbor at St. Petersburg would leave around the twenty-first of the month. This gave them about ten days in which to conclude the matter.

A few hours after the letter arrived at Count Nessel-

rode's offices, Baron de Brunnow, who was Nesselrode's
counselor, came to the American legation with some words
of advice. He asked Buchanan to rewrite the letter so that
it would not appear that Nesselrode had prompted the
matter.

Nesselrode had been unduly optimistic. The matter
could not be settled before the last steamboat left and the
ice closed in on Russia.

The Count asked Buchanan to be careful that no other
diplomats in St. Petersburg discovered that negotiations
for a trade treaty were in progress, for this might give
Count Cancrene additional ammunition to put an end to
the project. The negotiations continued, and Buchanan
was very careful not to reveal any information, although
the diplomats of St. Petersburg were constantly probing.
Finally, Count Nesselrode said the Czar would accept the
treaty. Buchanan suggested that it be signed on December
18, the Czar's fête day. Nesselrode agreed, and the matter
was settled.

Then, at a diplomatic reception, the Czar disclosed what
had been up to that point the best kept secret of the season.
Buchanan had come to St. Petersburg with only a frag-
mentary knowledge of French, and at his first reception by
the Czar it had been necessary to employ the services of an
interpreter. But Buchanan had progressed in the use of the
language, and towards the middle of December he was
fluent enough that he could carry on conversation with
Count Nesselrode without an interpreter.

The Czar evidently did not know of Buchanan's linguis-
tic progress, and at this particular reception, as Buchanan
was presented to the court, he spoke to the American minister loudly in French and then immediately called for an
interpreter.

The foreign diplomatic corps was lined up according to

the protocol of the day, which meant that the diplomatic representative of a sovereign nation who had personally been longest in St. Petersburg was the leading or senior diplomat. The English had just sent a new ambassador, Mr. Bligh, to represent them, and, although the English ambassador was more important than the American minister, Buchanan had been in St. Petersburg longer than Bligh, so he stood just above him in the line. When the Czar called for an interpreter, he immediately looked at Ambassador Bligh, who shared a language with the American.

"I signed the order yesterday that the treaty should be executed according to your wishes," the Czar said pleasantly to Buchanan, in French. Then, remembering that Buchanan's French had been inadequate at their last meeting, he raised his voice, beckoned to British Ambassador Bligh, and repeated the message, asking the Englishman to translate.

Ambassador Bligh was astonished. Minister Buchanan was embarrassed. Prime Minister Nesselrode was chagrined. All of St. Petersburg was agog. What treaty? What kind of treaty? Just what had the Americans been up to in the past few months?

The reception buzzed with gossip. A few hours later, Buchanan learned that the Czar had not made a social gaffe, as he first thought, but that it was all planned. The British ambassador took Buchanan aside and asked him what kind of treaty it was. Buchanan had no hesitation in replying that it was a commercial treaty. Then he learned that the special mission of Lord Durham, who had spent the summer in Moscow, had been to conclude a commercial treaty between Russia and England, and that Durham had failed. The Czar was just rubbing the British wounds a little.

The treaty was signed. Even Count Cancrene soon made
it a point to tell Minister Buchanan that he favored the
treaty and that he had decided that the United States alone
among nations deserved such special consideration because of the American policy of non-involvement in the affairs of others.

Buchanan was also entrusted with the responsibility
of concluding a maritime treaty. The object of the treaty
was to safeguard United States ships in case of war between
other powers, and thus avoid repetition of the circumstances that brought about the War of 1812. Basically,
much of the friction between the United States and Britain
in the early part of the nineteenth century had been caused
by Britain's practice of stopping American ships to see if
they carried cargoes destined for Britain's enemies. The
American government wanted to be sure that the Russians would never stop American ships, even if Russia
were to go to war.

Count Nesselrode had no particular objection to such
a treaty, but during the period that Buchanan was in St.
Petersburg, Russian policy changed. The Russians became
no less friendly to the United States, but they were engaged
in delicate negotiations with England, and did not wish
to antagonize them. Nesselrode knew quite well that such
a treaty would upset the British because it would be a
criticism, in a way, of former British policy, and Britain,
which was the world's foremost sea power, would countenance nothing that threatened her ascendency on the
sea.

Just after the treaty of commerce was signed, there came
an unfortunate incident to disturb relations between the
United States and Russia. In 1831, the Czar's government
had put down the insurrection in Poland and had begun
the process of Russification of that country. This meant

the movement of whole populations, the destruction of political rights, and the dispatch of Russian administrators into Poland to rule with an iron hand.

In the United States, this policy was watched by some observers with great distress. The Washington *Globe* was the official newspaper of the administration in those days; that is to say, the *Globe* carried the government's legal advertising and was generally regarded as the newspaper in which the President would make policy statements if he chose to make them through the press. But Andrew Jackson did not control the *Globe,* although his influence upon it was considerable.

The *Globe* complained in print about the Russian policy in Poland. The Russian *chargé d'affaires,* Baron Sacken, took offense and assumed that the complaint represented the official policy of the United States government. He wrote a stiff note to the State Department.

Secretary of State Livingston informed the President of the note without showing it to him, and Jackson indicated that the Russian representative ought to withdraw it, rather than demand an answer to it. The note remained, however. After several months it was answered, but because it was not withdrawn, President Jackson insisted that Minister Buchanan make a protest to the foreign ministry in St. Petersburg about the conduct of the *chargé d'affaires* and the language of the note.

Buchanan paid a call on Count Nesselrode, who was as distressed about the disagreement as Buchanan. They talked, and the Count finally said that Baron Sacken was leaving Washington and that matters would be explained to the President to his satisfaction by the new ambassador. So the unpleasantness ended.

The real problem for the Russians in this argument was to understand how the American government could claim that the *Globe* was an "official" newspaper, yet disclaim responsibility for its actions. Indeed this was a problem, and eventually it led to the discontinuance of the policy of maintaining an "official" newspaper in a nation that was dedicated to freedom of speech and the press. Buchanan advised that at least the editor of the *Globe* ought to refrain from attacking the Emperor of Russia if the United States government wished to get anywhere in seeking special concessions from the Russians.

In the spring of 1833, James Buchanan received permission from President Jackson to return home when he felt he must. Buchanan wanted to go home. The winter had been long and trying. In May he wrote to friends that the Neva had been frozen for six months but that what he really suffered from was not the cold but the excessive heat of the houses in winter.

Buchanan had spent a difficult winter, the most difficult part being how to approach the problem of entertaining. He had no personal fortune, and the American government allowed him so little for his house and salary that he could scarcely afford to entertain at all. Consequently, he was the only foreign representative in St. Petersburg who did not have liveried servants, and when he held dinners they were simple affairs in what he called "plain republican style." However, these dinners caught the fancy of the Russian court, and Buchanan was not pitied or scorned but became an object of admiration, even at the royal court.

In the spring, Buchanan's friends wrote that he could be and ought to be elected to the United States Senate. Buchanan hoped this was true, although he did not dare hope too much. He was certain of one thing: after his experiences in Washington and now at the most splendid court in the world, he was quite spoiled for the practice of law in a small Pennsylvania town. He even considered moving to New York or Baltimore to attempt to rebuild his political fortunes in an atmosphere where there was more money and more society. The precedent for this, of course, lay in the career of Daniel Webster, who had left his native New Hampshire to practice law and then to become a political leader in Massachusetts.

In June, Buchanan made a trip to Moscow, which was almost entirely a sight-seeing visit. On his return, he waited eagerly for an opportunity to go home, but he also waited with some qualms, for he had the nagging feeling that his political career was about to come to an end and that there was nothing he could do about it.

In July, he learned that his mother had died in May. In a sense this removed one of the major reasons for his reluctance to remain in Russia. President Jackson had specifically alluded to Buchanan's mother in giving the Minister permission to leave St. Petersburg any time that he felt it necessary. But the die was cast. Buchanan had talked so much about going home that there was no question about his remaining. He departed after an audience with the Czar, who embraced him and told him to tell President Jackson to send to Russia another minister exactly like Buchanan.

So Buchanan set off on the voyage home. First he went to Cronstadt, the port of St. Petersburg, where he and several other travelers, including members of the Russian court, boarded the steamship "Alexandra," which traveled to Travemunde. The fare was $50, or 250 rubles, which he found very high and attributed to the granting, most unwisely, of a monopoly. It was a rough trip; the steamer was not powerful enough for her tonnage, and she could hardly move against the strong headwind.

After landing, the American minister went to Cologne, and from there to Aix-la-Chapelle, and then to Paris, where he spent several days sight-seeing. He called on Lafayette, but found that he was in the country, as were several other friends of America, all of them following the French custom of spending August away from the city's heat.

From Paris, Buchanan traveled to Rouen and then crossed the English Channel between Le Havre and Southampton, and took the train to London where he put up at Thompson's hotel in Cavendish Square. He dined at the house of Prince Lieven, the Russian ambassador, and at Lord Palmerston's. He met the glittering women and proud men of the world of London society on even terms, for he was a man of note now—President Jackson's Minister to Russia who had concluded the successful trade treaty.

Buchanan learned and exchanged the gossip of the day. He talked with Prince Talleyrand, the great French statesman; Prince Esterhazy, the Hungarian; Baron Bülow; and lesser dignitaries. They discussed the failings of the King of Holland and the superiority of the American shipbuilders over the English, and they talked of the foibles of the courts and the treaties between nations. Soon, however, these pleasant meetings ended and Minister James Buchanan went aboard his sailing ship for the long voyage home to the United States and an unknown future.

CHAPTER 4

Senator

JAMES BUCHANAN exercised considerable patience in the year that began in the autumn of 1833. Instead of moving from Lancaster to Baltimore or some other city, he remained in his home and occupied himself with his private affairs. He paid a call on the President, as was required of a returning diplomat, but then he retired from the foreign service of his country. It had never been expected that he would do otherwise; Buchanan told everyone, at home and abroad, that he was not a professional diplomat, nor did he aspire to become one.

In the summer of 1834 Buchanan served for several months as a member of a commission that was formed to regulate the use of the waters of the Delaware River. New Jersey and Pennsylvania both had an interest in this river, which forms their border. Each state chose several commissioners, and together they settled on the future of the river, for the moment at least.

In December of that year President Jackson selected Senator Wilkins of Pennsylvania to be the new Minister to Russia, and it became necessary for the Pennsylvania legislature to choose a new senator. From a field of four candidates, the legislators chose James Buchanan on the fourth ballot. In December, then, Buchanan went back to Washington.

These were great, if trying years in the United States Senate. Vice-President Martin van Buren was presiding officer. The Senate was dominated by the figures of Henry Clay, Daniel Webster, and John C. Calhoun.

Senator Buchanan immediately found himself engaged in an argument in the Senate on a subject about which he had special knowledge. It concerned a quarrel between the United States and France. The quarrel originated in an agreement between the two nations to settle claims of American citizens against France and of French citizens against the United States. All went well until it came time for France to make her first payment, and then her parliament refused to make an appropriation to meet the payment.

When Buchanan had passed through Paris in the summer of 1833, he had held informal discussions with several French statesmen about this problem, and he was well-informed on the question. Actually the matter did not involve the French government in power; King Louis Philippe was in favor of making the payments and so was much of the parliament, but the opposition was using the issue as a weapon in internal politics.

The affair nearly started a war—or so it seemed. In 1834, in his annual message to Congress, President Jackson spoke severely of the French default. (He had been encouraged to do so, it seems, by the French king himself.)

The President's message arrived in Paris early in January and created an unpleasant sensation. The French minister to the United States was recalled, and Minister Livingston was told that he was *persona non grata* at the French court. War seemed near. Indeed, Senator Buchanan spoke of the possibility of war as he discussed the hopes for settlement in one of his earliest speeches in the Senate.

There is a point, he said, at which diplomacy ends and a nation must abandon her rights or assert them by force.

"After having negotiated for a quarter of a century to obtain a treaty to redress the wrongs of our injured citizens, and after the French Chamber has once deliberately rejected that treaty, will not this point have been reached, should the Chamber again refuse to make the appropriation?" he asked. He suggested that the Senate resolve to inform France that the United States had reached just such a point. Then France would be forced to decide whether she wanted to go to war or to pay those claims which the executive branch of her government had determined to be just. This was the attitude of many in Congress, and consequently such a resolution was passed.

For several months it seemed that war with France was inevitable. The President recommended a policy of partial non-intercourse with France, the next thing to the severance of relations.

During the winter of 1835, the debate and the quarrel continued. Senators Clay and Webster, leaders of the emerging Whig coalition, opposed the administration's strong measures regarding France. Buchanan, ever a supporter of General Jackson, found himself defending the President even when there were signs of intemperance in the President's statements. The administration attempted to push through a measure calling for an increase in the armed forces of the nation, but the Whigs blocked it, saying that the quarrel with France was simply an excuse and that there was no need for further expenditure of federal funds for defense. The bill, called the fortification bill, did not pass, although Buchanan and other Democratic-Republican senators argued for it.

The Whigs continued to grow in strength. The movement had been formed in 1834, when Clay, Webster, and Calhoun joined forces, in an attempt to secure censure of President Jackson for his conduct in office. The censure motions had been passed before James Buchanan was elected to the Senate, but the repercussions were still being felt. Much of the ill-feeling stemmed from the personal ambitions of Calhoun and the other two leaders of the new coalition, but some of it was directly attributable to the lively struggle over the question of the national bank and the deposit of federal funds. Jackson had won the struggle in 1833 and 1834 with his firm refusal to accept a new national bank, and, in a sense, James Buchanan was personally affected by the outcome. Having failed to obtain a new federal charter, the Bank of the United States became the Bank of the United States of Pennsylvania, after securing a charter in that state.

Following the censure of the President for his official actions, Jackson's friends in the Senate attempted to protect him, while the enemy Whigs tried to destroy the President's influence wherever they could. One of the important issues was the right of removal of officials from the executive departments. President Jackson had removed a number of appointed officials, including a Secretary of the Treasury, in arguments over the national banking proposition. The Whigs took the position that he had no right to remove officials without giving reasonable explanations; the Jackson supporters took the position that, as an elected chief executive, the President had the right to operate the executive branch of government as he saw fit, subject to the will of the people only.

In February, 1835, Senator Buchanan took an active part in defense of this Jackson position, both in speeches on the floor of the Senate and in committee work and discussion with other senators off the floor.

This year and during the next two years the political battle between the Whigs and the Democrats became exceedingly vigorous. Senator Benton of Missouri, a Democrat, introduced legislation to expunge the censure of Jackson from the records of the Senate, and in 1837 this was finally achieved, through voting that was almost entirely along party lines. In the course of the discussions, Senator Buchanan made several addresses. One in particular pointed to the personal nature of the attack on the President and the dangers, constitutionally speaking, of allowing personal politics to influence the relationship between Congress and the chief executive. In the end, the censure of 1834 was expunged from the records of the United States Senate. The journal of the Senate was turned back to 1834, and it was written into the pages that the action had been rescinded.

James Buchanan entered the United States Senate and his entire career in that legislative body was spent during the period of the growing heat of feeling on the subject of slavery. Buchanan's attitudes toward slavery were a matter of record: he detested slavery, but he could see no way for the United States to rid herself of the evil. Personally, he was partial to southerners. He liked their manners, he liked their way of speech, and he liked their style of entertaining. He was of Scotch-Irish descent, and so were many of the southerners he met. The southerners appealed to him because he had grown accustomed to people of good manners and gentle deportment during the period he served as ambassador. He discovered that he liked the social amenities, and the people of the South were much better versed in them than the people he knew in the North.

Yet Buchanan was not blind to the shortcomings of his southern friends. He once told an acquaintance that he did not believe any southern scholar would ever complete a

biography of Thomas Jefferson because southerners did
not have the perseverence for such exacting work. Buchanan knew they were hot-tempered and inclined toward
precipitous action.

Early in 1836 petitions began to come into Congress ad-
vocating the abolition of slavery in the District of Columbia. This was the abolitionists' way of drawing the attention of Congress to the national problem, or what they regarded as a national problem. Congress ruled over the District of Columbia, acting in that sense as a city government.
But any action taken by Congress that would affect the
District of Columbia would be deemed to represent congressional policy at large. Thus, southerners to whom the
matter of slavery in the District of Columbia was of no con-
cern at all were forced to oppose the abolition of slavery
and slave trading there in the interest of preserving the
right of southern states to maintain slavery.

Two petitions came to the Senate in January, 1836, and
Senator Calhoun of South Carolina first insisted that they
be read and then objected to their being accepted for consideration by Congress.

Senator Buchanan arose in the Senate to state his position on slavery, prompted by a memorial he had received
from the Society of Friends, or Quakers, who were so
prominent in the affairs of his state.

Congress had no right or power over slavery in the states
where it existed, he said, and that matter had been
thoroughly settled in a number of constitutional studies
by the Supreme Court. Slavery existed before the Union
was formed, and, in adopting the Constitution, the various
states did not give the federal government the right to interfere with their way of life or their property rights in
slaves.

The Constitution, he said, recognized the right of slave

property by prohibiting any state from discharging a runaway slave from bondage and by giving the slave states representation in Congress based on all of the free persons and in proportion to three-fifths of the number of slaves.

Further, he said, the issue had been dealt with by the First Congress of the United States in 1790. The Pennsylvania Society for the Abolition of Slavery had brought up a memorial in February of that year. On March 23 the House of Representatives, sitting as a committee of the whole, had passed the following resolution:

That Congress have no authority to interfere in the emancipation of slaves, or in the treatment of them within any of the states; it remaining with the several states alone to provide any regulations therein, which humanity and true policy may require.

Senator Buchanan said that in the abstract his views on slavery were those of the people of Pennsylvania—he was opposed to slavery. But whatever his opinions as a person, he would never attempt to help violate the fundamental concept as set down in the Constitution.

"The Union will be dissolved, and incalculable evils will arise from its ashes," he said, "the moment any such attempt is seriously made by the free states in Congress."

This was Senator James Buchanan's mature view of the problem of slavery in the United States, and it accounts, in large part, for Buchanan's successes and failures in public office in the years to come. He never relaxed this view; personally abhorring slavery, he could see no way that it could be abolished legally and rightly, given the conditions under which the southern states originally entered the Union. As a lawyer, he looked at the problem as one of law primarily. Certainly he never looked upon slavery with the eyes of a revolutionary or a reformer, because he was neither of these. He was a Pennsylvania gentleman, the son of a well-to-do farmer. He had raised himself, through his own efforts, to the point where he consorted with presidents, princes, and kings. He was proud of his record, proud of the republic in which he lived, where a man could so raise himself. He regarded himself as a gentleman, and he was gentle in manner and cultivated in speech. The concept that the South could be told to abolish slavery and then be beaten into submission was entirely foreign to his nature. He could see no *reasonable* way of abolishing slavery; therefore he believed it could never be abolished. The thought of violence was entirely foreign to his nature; at the worst, he believed, the North would force the South into secession, and then the future of the various states would be much in doubt because the states would be left prey to the ambitions of strong European nations.

He abhorred slavery, but he abhorred the efforts of the abolitionists as much. "These fanatics," he called them. He said that the abolitionists actually harmed the cause of the slaves they tried to help because in all the agitation the masters felt it necessary to "tighten the reins of authority over their slaves" and thus did not grant indulgences which they would otherwise give cheerfully.

Buchanan nonetheless supported the right of the Society of Friends to petition Congress for the abolition of slavery in the District of Columbia, on the grounds that citizens of the Republic must always have the right to petition Congress and Congress must listen to their petitions. Senator Calhoun demanded that petitions on the matter of slavery be disregarded and rejected without consideration.

Buchanan's position, again, was dictated by his regard for law and the Constitution. When the voting came on March 9, 1836, Buchanan and thirty-five other senators voted to receive the petition of the Society of Friends in

Philadelphia, and Senator Calhoun and nine other south-erners voted against receiving it.

Having secured the right to petition thus, Buchanan then moved that the petition be rejected. He repeated his arguments and strengthened them. Slavery, he said, was the weak point among American institutions.

Tariffs may be raised almost to prohibition, and then they may be reduced so as to yield an adequate protection to the manufacturer; our Union is sufficiently strong to endure the shock. Fierce political storms may arise—the moral elements of the country may be convulsed by the struggles of ambitious men for the highest honors of the government—the sunshine does not more certainly succeed the storm, than that all will again be peace. Touch this question of slavery seriously—let it once be made manifest to the people of the South that they cannot live with us, except in a state of continual apprehension and alarm for their wives and their children, for all that is near and dear to them upon the earth—and the Union is from that moment dissolved. It does not then become a question of expediency, but of self-preservation. It is a question brought home to the fireside, to the domestic circle of every white man in the southern states. This day, this dark and gloomy day for the Republic, will, I most devoutly trust and believe, never arrive. Although, in Pennsylvania, we are opposed to slavery in the abstract, yet we will never violate the constitutional compact which we have made with our sister states. Their rights will be held sacred by us. Under the Constitution, it is their own question; and there let it remain.

The issue of slavery arose again in 1836 when President Jackson asked Congress to pass a law to prevent the use of the mails for the circulation of incendiary publications—particularly those relating to slavery which abolition groups were beginning to send through the mails all around the country. The bill, as presented, specifically outlawed the circulation of material touching on slavery in states and

territories where the circulation of such material was prohibited, as in the South.

Daniel Webster from Massachusetts argued against the
bill, saying it abridged the freedom of speech and the
press. Buchanan replied. He said that the only states to
which this law applied were those slave states where the
danger of slave insurrections had grown so large, because
of the efforts of the abolitionists, that laws had been passed
forbidding material to be circulated on the problem of
slavery. The public had no right to send publications
through the post office that would be aimed at inciting war
or insurrection, he said.

Henry Clay said he thought the bill was totally unneces-
sary since the states involved had dealt with the problem
in their own way, and that the law would give huge new
powers to the Postmaster-General and would violate the
Constitution. Further, he noted, a non-slave state might
prohibit defenses of slavery and therefore add to the confusion and the ills of the law. Senator Calhoun added his
opinion that the only value of this law was that it would
"cause the federal authorities to abstain" from violating
the laws of the states.

Each opinion was a reflection of the man who made it:
Webster was concerned with the basic constitutional question of freedom of speech; Buchanan was convinced that
the Constitution forbade the Congress from meddling with
slavery in the sense of trying to destroy it; Clay wanted the
states to work out their own problems without interference
of any kind from the federal government; and Calhoun
was the staunch advocate of states' rights, holding that the
federal government had no right to talk about laws that
would overlap or contradict the laws of the states.

On the basis that the law was aimed at keeping federal
authorities from putting their noses into state business,

Calhoun voted for it. Buchanan voted for it because he wanted to keep the abolitionists from stirring up trouble, and, besides, he was an administration man. Clay and Webster voted against the bill, each for his separate reason, and in the final vote the bill was defeated 25–19.

Senator Buchanan was no man's creature, however. When the Texas question arose in the Senate in the spring of 1836 and a number of petitioners and senators wanted to recognize the independence of Texas, which was rebelling against Mexico, Buchanan said that although his heart went out to the Texans, there could be no doubt in his mind that Texas was a province of Mexico.

After 1837, Buchanan was acknowledged as a leader of the Democratic party within the Senate, and he often engaged in vigorous debate with Henry Clay and Daniel Webster on matters that divided the Democrats and these Whigs. He transferred his loyalty from Jackson to Van Buren when the New Yorker was selected by Jackson as his successor and became the Democratic candidate for President in 1836. Buchanan did not support Van Buren without qualms, however. He feared that Van Buren, the consummate politician, would be so interested in putting together political elements that he would not show the firmness and certainty of judgment that were necessary to the Presidency. He wrote as much to President Jackson, but Jackson calmed his fears, saying that Van Buren would prove to be a man of strong judgment.

Late in the 1830s, the question of the national bank and the financial policy of the government continued in importance. The old United States national bank, which was operating in Philadelphia as a state bank, tried to renew its power and to make some extra profits by a most improper speculation. The bank reissued some of the old notes of the United States national bank. With these notes the Philadelphia bankers bought up currency issued by local southern banks, taking huge discounts because the local bank currency was not worth its face value. (Since the banks could not afford to redeem their paper money in gold or silver, the people had lost confidence in the money.) The Bank of the United States of Pennsylvania then used the cheap southern money to buy cotton, speculated with the cotton in the markets of Europe, and made additional profits. The people in the South who accepted these reissued notes thought they were really dealing with a currency backed by the United States government. The profits to the Pennsylvania bank were immense. Senator Buchanan flayed the bankers and urged Congress to make it illegal for banks to speculate in commodities, as the Philadelphia bank had done.

To prevent this meddling with the currency—and sometimes with public funds—the loyal Jacksonians suggested the establishment of an independent United States treasury, which would hold the money collected by the government in taxes and would issue its own paper money. The paper would be issued only to facilitate business transactions. It was difficult to carry $1,000 in gold or silver around in one's pocket, but simple enough to carry $1,000 in notes that could be redeemed in gold or silver at the treasury. By guaranteeing that the money could be redeemed in gold or silver, this paper money would be as good as gold—as long as the government lived up to its promise.

Many people had lost faith in the private banks because they, too, had promised to redeem their paper notes with metal money when asked, but when they fell into difficulties at the end of the War of 1812, they refused to do so. The government might have closed these banks for their failure to live up to their promises, but most were state

banks, which were regulated jealously by the state governments, and to close them down when there was any chance
that they might some day pay their debts would have been
to work real hardship on the people who could afford it
least—the small merchants, small landholders, and workers who had limited assets and depended heavily on their
cash supplies. The rich, whose holdings were varied and
vast, would have been virtually unaffected.

The treasury issue became vital with the Panic of 1837.
The effects of the panic lasted for five years, and in some
areas of the United States business was virtually paralyzed
during much of the time. Until 1837, expansion had been
on the minds of most Americans, and public lands were sell-
ing rapidly as settlers and speculators moved into the
western country. But in two short years, after 1836, the sale
of public lands fell from 20,000,000 to 3,500,000 acres.

The Democrats controlled the Twenty-sixth Congress
that met in 1840, and they passed the Independent Treasury
Act, which had been hotly debated for three years.

Then came the presidential campaign of 1840. President
Van Buren was the accepted candidate of the Democrats to
succeed himself. The Whigs passed over Henry Clay and
nominated William Henry Harrison of Ohio, the military
hero of the unnamed war against the western Indians
under Tecumseh, which ended in the victory at Tippe-
canoe, Indiana.

The country was tired of considering troublesome political issues, General Harrison had the fatherly appeal of a
military man, and President Van Buren had antagonized
many people because he was so apparently the master politician, using patronage and influence to strengthen the
Democratic party.

Van Buren had many fine qualities as a political leader
and statesman; William Henry Harrison had neither po-

litical nor governmental experience outside the military organization. Still, in the wave of emotionalism and reaction against three years of hard times, all these facts were forgotten and Harrison swept through the key states, winning 270 electoral votes and carrying nineteen of the twenty-six states. The popular vote was much closer; Harrison really carried only about 150,000 more votes all across the country than Van Buren's 1,128,702, but Harrison had these 150,000 votes in the right states, and so the electoral victory seemed great although the voting was very close.

From the standpoint of party politics, it was the most startling change in the history of the Republic. The Whig movement was not a party at all. It was made up of southern slaveholders and northern abolitionists, those who favored paper money and those who favored the use of gold and silver, men who wanted free trade and others who wanted high protective tariffs. The Whigs, one might say, were united only in their opposition to the Democratic party of General Jackson and Martin Van Buren. The defeat was startling in many ways, not the least of them the fact that the Democrats carried only one large state, Virginia, and even Van Buren's New York and Jackson's Tennessee went to the Whigs.

Senator Buchanan was fortunate that he did not have to stand for his own seat because he might easily have been ousted, too. But he did not have to run; he had been reelected by the legislature in 1837 to a full six-year term. Shortly before the election, Buchanan rejected an offer from President Van Buren to join the cabinet as Attorney-General. He preferred at that time to remain in the Senate, perhaps because he saw indications in his own state of Pennsylvania that the national party was not faring well.

Harrison was elected, but he barely served a month as President before he died and Vice-President John Tyler assumed the job as first executive. Since the Whigs held control of both houses of Congress, they attempted to pass legislation creating a new Bank of the United States, and they discarded the treasury system established by the Democrats.

But the looseness of the Whig confederation was its own undoing as a governing body. John Tyler happened to oppose the establishment of a national bank, and when the bill was sent to him for signature he vetoed it, much to the amazement and anger of Henry Clay and other Whigs. In August and September, 1841, the struggle was fought between the Whigs of Congress and the White House. In the Senate, the Whigs tried, and failed, to override the presidential veto by securing a two-thirds majority vote. After conferring with President Tyler, the Whigs presented another bill, but not all of the President's conditions were met, and the second bill to establish a fiscal bank of the United States was defeated. Again, the Whigs could not override the veto.

This was the end of the Whig coalition in governing the nation under President Tyler. No Congress had been as unresponsive to the President's wishes as this Congress became since the days of John Quincy Adams in the White House. All the members of the cabinet resigned except Daniel Webster, who stayed on as Secretary of State.

In the Senate, James Buchanan engaged in several clashes with Henry Clay, over the bank bills and over a bill that would allow any person in the United States to take bankruptcy if he found that his debts had become intolerable. Buchanan, true to the principles he had brought with him to the House of Representatives twenty years earlier, still opposed the bankruptcy bill because he felt it would enable unscrupulous traders to escape payment of just debts.

In a way, it might be valuable to examine Buchanan's

reasoning, for it is the same variety of reasoning that he brought to bear on the slavery question. In the first place, he said, the complex machinery established in the bill to deal with bankruptcy would make it impossible for the courts to do as the law commanded. They could not handle the work; it would take ten times as many courts to handle the work. He was arguing, here, against the proponents of the measure who claimed that the hardships of the recent depression had created a half million bankrupts in the United States, men desperate for relief from intolerable debt. Now, there were not a half million bankrupts, and Buchanan knew it. His argument was as specious, although logically correct, as were the arguments of the bill's backers. In other words, he was as willing as the next man to stray from the actual point in order to agree with logic. The logic, for example, of his position on the issue of slavery was unassailable, if one were to accept the theory that the nation's basic law was unchangeable. Had that been true, and had the narrow thinkers been able to hold the remainder of the nation to the position that nothing could be done about slavery because the slave states existed when they entered the Union—then indeed in 1861 the union of the states would have had to be dissolved or the Constitution of the United States would have had to be scrapped and a new, equally unchangeable basic law enacted. This would have lent itself to the iron-like firmness that characterized the French system for two hundred years under the Republic and led to violent change after violent change.

James Buchanan was not alone in his position or in his ways of thinking. He opposed the bankruptcy bill, although he was sympathetic to poor bankrupts. He wanted to do something for them, but he claimed that nothing could be done, and, like many of the men of his time, he was willing to let it go at that, taking refuge from his conscience in the rigidity of the law. He did pay lip-service to the concept of a bankruptcy law, but he was unwilling to offer an alternative to the measure before the Senate, contenting himself with vague generalities. Also, he was always concerned with the rights and responsibilities of the states to pass such legislation. Here again, the concept of states' rights was very strong in Buchanan's mind. His good will was unmistakable, and so was his dedication to a narrow interpretation of the Constitution.

As the days of the Tyler administration continued, it became apparent that if Tyler wished to make any progress at all some accommodation would have to be reached between the President and the Democratic party. Tyler was so much at odds with the Whigs that nothing else could be done. Buchanan's friend and political ally, James Porter, was made Secretary of War in 1843, and Buchanan began to lean more toward the administration. He had already supported Tyler in an important fight on the floor of the Senate over the right of the President to veto legislation.

Henry Clay and other Whigs became so angered at Tyler during the debates over the fiscal national bank, which they had expected to bring to such quick and easy life, that Clay brought forth a constitutional amendment which would have destroyed the veto power. The amendment required only a bare majority of the votes in both houses of Congress to override the President's veto. This represented a great change. Obviously, if a bill could be passed by both houses and sent to the President for signature, the same bill could be passed again, and thus the President's veto would amount to nothing at all. Buchanan claimed that Henry Clay had more than one motive in offering the legislation. Clay was again seeking the nomination of the

Whigs for 1844, and the veto question would give him an excellent popular issue. The idea of a national bank and the possibility of increased credit and cheap paper money appealed to many voters, and Clay hoped to present himself as the champion of the people against the "interests" thus.

Again, a part of Buchanan's political philosophy, which was to have so much bearing on the national course a few years later, was made known in his speech in reply to Henry Clay on the question of the presidential veto.

This matter struck deep at the heart of America's basic law, he said. The veto power was one of the most effective safeguards of the Union, and a way of carrying into effect the will of the people. No veto had ever been overruled, he pointed out, because the President had never vetoed a measure unless he was certain that he was right and would be sustained by the people in his veto. In fifty years the presidential veto had been exercised only twenty times; out of a total of six thousand bills passed, only twenty acts of Congress had been disapproved by the President. The important vetoes had been those of Washington, Madison, Jackson, and Tyler, and all but Washington's had concerned three basic subjects: the banking system, public lands, and internal improvements. Washington's veto, which Buchanan regarded as the most questionable of all the vetoes, concerned the reduction of the standing army of the United States. Both houses of Congress voted to reduce the armed forces, but Washington vetoed the measure.

It is possible that at some future day the majority in Congress may attempt, by indirect means, to emancipate the slaves in the South. There is no knowing through what channel the ever active spirit of fanaticism may seek to accomplish its object. The attempt may be made through the taxing power or through some other express power granted by the Constitution. God only knows how it may be made. It is hard to say what means fanaticism may not adopt to accomplish its purpose. Do we feel so secure, in this hour of peril from abroad and peril at home, as to be willing to prostrate any of the barriers which the Constitution has reared against hasty and dangerous legislation? No, sir, never was the value of the veto power more manifest than at the present moment. For the weaker portion of the Union, whose constitutional rights are now assailed with such violence, to think of abandoning this safeguard, would be almost suicidal. It is my solemn conviction, that there never was a wiser or more beautiful adaptation of theory to practice in any government than that which requires a majority of two-thirds in both houses of Congress to pass an act returned by the President with his objections, under all the high responsibilities which he owes to his country.

So Buchanan continued to espouse his own manner of interpreting the Constitution. He was most consistent in his actions.

In 1844 the Democrats nominated James K. Polk for the Presidency, and the Whigs nominated Henry Clay again. Clay considered the idea of bringing up his previous friendship with Buchanan, and of indicating, by dredging up a conversation of twenty years previous, that Buchanan had been an emissary of General Jackson, trying to get Clay's support for the Presidency in the election of 1824-25, which went to the House of Representatives. Buchanan proved himself an apt student of political affairs in assessing Clay's position. It was too bad, he said, that Clay had ever taken the position as Adams' Secretary of State, for it had ruined his chances of winning the Presidency. If he had not done so, Buchanan said, Clay would have been in retirement already, rather than running for office in 1844, and he would have retired after eight years in the White House. As it stood, Buchanan had every hope for the election of Polk.

Buchanan supported Polk quite wholeheartedly. At the convention in Baltimore there was some support for Buchanan himself when the first ballot drew near, but it was not the kind of support that nominates a candidate, and Buchanan sensed this and withdrew his name rapidly, before anyone could be annoyed or angered. The Pennsylvania legislature had asked Buchanan to run for President in 1843, and had offered to endorse his candidacy, but he refused. He was much more pleased at being elected to the United States Senate by that legislature, for the third time. Not that he was unambitious or spurned the Presidency. Not at all. He simply recognized the political facts of life: that he was not the man for the nomination that year and that if he sought it he would be running against Van Buren and other prominent Democrats who were quite capable of promoting party discord. He did say, just before the convention, that if Van Buren withdrew or could not be nominated, his name could be used; however, he was not eager or responsive to those who might have supported him, and he came out of the convention with honor, but Polk came out with the nomination.

When the election of 1844 came, James K. Polk was elected, and he carried Pennsylvania, much to Buchanan's delight. Buchanan wrote to Polk, telling him that if the candidate had been Martin Van Buren, then Henry Clay would have won in Pennsylvania.

Buchanan was a member of the Senate Committee on Foreign Relations, and he had devoted a considerable amount of time to study of American problems abroad. The

most important of these in the 1840's was the Texas question, for the sentiment for (and against) the annexation of
Texas was very strong indeed. The Texas question was com-
plicated since Texas, the republic, was a slaveholding nation. Further, urged on by the British, the Mexicans had indicated that if Texas was annexed to the United States, the
action would mean war between Mexico and this country.

One of the arguments raised in Congress was that new
states could not be admitted to the Union unless they had
arisen from within territory controlled by the United
States. This meant, if followed, that the United States could
never annex another independent nation. Buchanan, with
what was either masterly indirection for political purposes
or monumental obtuseness, refused to deal with the merits
of Texas annexation, but rather dedicated his efforts in
discussion to consideration of the constitutional question:
could independent states be annexed to the Union?

Others were not so vague or so bland. On the first day of
March, 1845, joint resolutions calling for the annexation
of Texas were adopted in Congress. These resolutions
called for the admission of Texas into the Union as a slave
state. They called also for the possible formation of four
more states out of this territory, and the future admission
of these as either slave or free states—depending on the
will of the people in the territory—if these states were
formed below the line of 36° 30'. That line of latitude had
been established in the Missouri Compromise as the point
above which no slavery would be permitted. The vote was
quite close; twenty-seven votes for the admission of Texas
and twenty-five votes against were cast in the Senate. True
to his principles in the past, Buchanan had refused to support the Texas bid for independence with armed force from
the United States. He had called attention, nearly a decade

earlier when the fight was in progress, to the traditional
neutrality of the United States, when the Spanish colonies
were rebelling against the European motherland.

. . . The Spanish provinces, throughout the whole continent of
America, had raised the standard of rebellion against the king of
Spain. They were struggling for liberty against oppression. The feelings of the American people were devotedly enlisted in their favor.
Our ardent wishes and our prayers for their success continued
throughout the whole long and bloody conflict. But we took no other
part in their cause, and we rendered them no assistance, except the
strong moral influence exerted over the world by our well-known
feelings and opinions in their favor. When did we recognize their independence? Not till after they had achieved it by their arms; not
until the contest was over, and victory had perched upon their ban-
ners; not until the good fight had been fought and won. We then led
the van in acknowledging their independence. But until they were
independent in fact, we resisted every effort and every eloquent appeal which was made in their behalf, to induce us to depart from the
settled policy of the country. When the fact of their actual independence was established, then, and not till then, did we acknowl-
edge it.

This was the American position, following a tradition
established by George Washington almost on the birth of
the nation. It continued, really, to be the American policy
until the beginning of World War II, although in the
Mexican situation that policy was overwhelmed by other
considerations. Buchanan was not simply obtuse, he was a
conservative Constitutionalist of the same stamp as many
southerners. Buchanan's personal sympathies were all
against slavery and the establishment of cruelty or tyranny
anywhere. He held, however, that although slavery and
tyranny were wrong the United States did not have any
moral right to destroy these institutions when such destruc-

tion meant the violation of the spirit of the Constitution or other laws of the nation. The position would be difficult to understand or sustain a century and a quarter after the beginning of the Civil War, but it was not an uncommon one in the 1830's and 1840's.

Buchanan adopted the position of President Polk and the Democratic majority in 1845—it was essential that he do so and quite normal because when President Polk formed his cabinet he looked at the election returns in Pennsylvania and listened to Buchanan's Pennsylvania friends, and then he appointed James Buchanan as Secretary of State.

CHAPTER 5

Secretary of State

JAMES K. POLK had come to the Presidency under unusual circumstances, or so it seemed to many of the Democrats and Whigs of the time. One of Buchanan's Whig friends, when told that Polk was the candidate of the Democrats, was stopped short. "My God, not Polk!" he said, indicating that the Whigs would have a very easy victory at the polls.

But Polk represented strength in the Democratic party at a time when the party was threatened by serious quarrels. John Calhoun, for example, had deserted the Democratic party to become Tyler's Secretary of State. There were other ambitious men: Martin Van Buren had not given up hope for a second term in the White House and Lewis Cass, the senator from Michigan, was a strong contender. Polk had the support of old General Jackson, and the campaign itself proved Jackson right. Polk reunited the Democratic party that had threatened to fall apart, and that had, in fact, so far disintegrated in 1840 that the Tennessee of Jackson and Polk had gone Whig. Polk was popular for another reason than the obvious one as man-in-the-middle. He had declared that he would not be a candidate to succeed himself.

This declaration also had a bearing on his attitude

towards James Buchanan. Polk did not trust Buchanan wholeheartedly. This was not unusual. Few political leaders ever trust one another wholly, particularly when they reach the top echelons of their party, for in any given four years there can be only one President, and once men's minds are fixed on the Presidency, the desire is like an illness and it overcomes all other ambition.

Polk was an anomaly; he was not excessively ambitious, and he entered the Presidency determined to remain in the post for only one term. Around him, then, he wanted men who would devote themselves wholeheartedly to the problems of the nation and not to the problems of politics. So, when he offered the State Department post to James Buchanan, Polk did so on the condition that Buchanan would resign from the cabinet if he became a candidate for the Presidency. This warning was directed at others as well, but it was put down in a letter to Buchanan.

James Buchanan was quite frank in his reply to the President-elect.

> I do not know that I shall ever desire to be a candidate for the Presidency. Most certainly I never yet strongly felt such an indication, and I have been willing and should at this moment be willing to accept a station which would, in my estimation of what is proper, deprive me of any prospect of reaching that office. Still, I could not, and would not, accept the high and honorable office to which you have called me at the expense of self-ostracism. My friends would unanimously condemn me were I to pursue this course. I cannot proclaim to the world that in no contingency shall I be a candidate for the Presidency in 1848. . . .

Buchanan could, however, promise that he would not exert himself to achieve the nomination as long as he was a member of Polk's cabinet, and he did so promise. He could promise that he would retire from the cabinet if nominated without actively seeking the nomination.

So the bargain was struck, a fair enough bargain, if somewhat restrictive on Buchanan and the other members of the cabinet, and James Buchanan became Secretary of State.

When James Buchanan assumed the powers of that office, he and the President faced two basic questions of foreign policy. One was the Oregon question, the determination of the boundary between the territory claimed by the United States and that claimed by Britain as a part of the Canada territory. The other important question was the annexation of Texas.

In 1827 Britain and the United States agreed, somewhat uncomfortably, to put the problem off for a few years. They did so by deciding then on a policy of "joint occupation." This policy worked well enough as long as there were few settlers in the region, but when men with plows began to displace men with traps, the settlers became uneasy about their own claims and land rights, and men on both sides agitated for settlement of the boundary.

The Americans claimed the land as far north as the southern point of Russian territory—which is now Alaska. This claim included all of western British Columbia, as far east as the Rocky Mountains. The British claimed the same territory and the area south as far as the Columbia River, which included the entire state of Washington and parts of what are now Montana and Idaho.

During the election campaign, President Polk's adherents talked loudly about the northern limits. "Fifty-four forty or fight" was a popular campaign slogan; the slogan meant that the United States would have all of the Oregon Territory or a war with Great Britain. Fortunately, although the public position was not changed, President Polk had no intention of holding out for so wild a claim. To insist on the claim would have been to ensure war with Britain, for it would have cut off the Canadian colonies from access to the Pacific Ocean, and this would have been intolerable.

President Polk and Secretary Buchanan recognized the practical impossibility of the American claim, and shortly after the inauguration they settled down to try to negotiate a true settlement of the long-standing dispute. In July, 1845, Polk authorized Secretary Buchanan to offer the 49th parallel as a boundary.

Meanwhile, in Congress the demands for settlement based on the American claim were growing. A resolution which terminated the joint United States-British occupation of the territory was offered in the House in January, 1846, and after considerable debate it was passed by both houses and signed by the President. On May 21, President Polk informed the British government that the occupation would end in a year.

However, when he had received the American offer, Richard Pakenham, the British Minister to the United States, viewed this action as a sign of American weakness. Without even asking London what he ought to do, the British minister rejected the American proposal out of hand, on July 30, 1845. This rejection created a wild roar of disapproval in the United States and strengthened the previous demand for "fifty-four forty or fight."

Secretary of State Buchanan wanted to continue to negotiate with the British, but Polk did not. And so, in the autumn of 1845, when the American annexation of Texas was in progress, negotiations with the British were broken off and it appeared that the United States was bent on grabbing all the territory around its borders—north, south, and west.

The demands for all the land to the Alaskan border were repeated, and American settlers pressed for physical control of the territory.

The autumn of 1845 might easily have brought war between the United States and Britain. In a way, conditions were ripe. The British had been lingering on the edges of the American-Mexican dispute over Texas, attempting to keep the United States from taking over Texas, and perhaps even more Mexican territory—as the British were afraid the Americans wished to do. Minister Pakenham's note of refusal on the 49th parallel offer was badly phrased; it indicated that the American position in demanding 54° 40′ was absurd and called on the American government to give the British their way.

Had Pakenham's refusal become public knowledge at the time, the demands in the United States would certainly have been for war. But Buchanan did not make the note public, and Polk backed him, although he refused to reopen negotiations in the face of such an insult.

Secretary Buchanan then began to work behind the scenes to secure a settlement. He wrote to the American minister in London and told him that he ought to lay the American position before the British foreign office.

Then Buchanan wrote to Minister Pakenham in Washington, reaffirming the American claim to 54°40′, and showing in detail how and why the United States could make such a demand. The 49th parallel settlement plan was withdrawn.

Too late, Minister Pakenham discovered that the American offer of a few months earlier had been very generous by American standards, and he asked that it be renewed. President Polk refused to renew the offer, and when Congress assembled in December the push for the whole of western Canada began.

It seemed as though the negotiations had reached an impasse. Secretary Buchanan asked the American minister in London to see if the British government would not reopen the question, thus preserving the American dignity. The correspondence between Pakenham and the American government was made public in the winter of 1846, and the feelings it aroused led to the demand that the joint occupation be ended.

Buchanan met several times with Minister Pakenham. On one occasion he suggested that if the question were to be arbitrated, as the British suggested, the arbitrator should be the Pope. Since both nations were heretic in their belief and attitude towards religion, they could be assured of just treatment. Minister Pakenham took the suggestion seriously, and Buchanan was hard put to persuade the British minister that he had been joking. They talked, also, of some of the serious problems that affected and might hinder the settlement, and since they were alone they talked as frankly as diplomats sometimes do.

Pakenham said the British objected to the grantings of lands to settlers in Oregon by the American government because this made the settlement between the two countries more difficult. He said this action violated the treaty; in addition he had heard the American government was going to appropriate money for the erection of forts by the settlers in the area, which again was a violation of the treaty. Buchanan replied that he had not thought much about the land grants because they had not yet been made. As far as the forts were concerned, he said, Mr. Pakenham ought to remember that all the Americans proposed to do was to build forts of the kind that the Hudson's Bay Company had already built in the area for the British settlers and trappers.

Pakenham asked why the settlers did not build their own forts as the Hudson's Bay Company had done, without government assistance. Buchanan reminded Pakenham that for all practical purposes the Hudson's Bay Company *was* the government and that the American settlers were too poor to build forts themselves.

Buchanan then said that both he and Pakenham knew

that all this trouble was caused by the Hudson's Bay Company. Were it not for the company, Buchanan said, the British would not care about giving up the rights to the territory, even to the point of 54°40′, which the Americans claimed. Pakenham replied that the company had rights in the Oregon Territory which had to be protected. (This was a silent admission that what Buchanan said was true.) Pakenham went on to say that the British government was so eager to get rid of the problem that no one cared if the arbitrator awarded the whole territory to the Americans. Buchanan said he believed this; he knew that the British "always played the lion, and never the fox." Pakenham said that Britain wanted peace, but he thought the United States wanted war. Why? Buchanan asked. What would the United States want to fight Britain about? Would not British naval superiority give them command of the Oregon coast? That was quite right, Pakenham said, but the war would not be confined to Oregon. If it could be, he would be very glad to fight it out with the Americans within the Oregon Territory and there alone.

Of course there was no such frankness in public, and such matters as war were not openly discussed. Diplomats could be honest with one another sitting across a table, but the demands of statements and positions for the public were another matter.

The public—the American public—was the problem here. The agitation about Texas, about California, and other areas in the American southwest had brought American emotions to a high pitch. The policy followed by President Polk, begun by Jackson really, was called "Manifest Destiny"; it referred to the expansion of the United States from shore to shore of its major continental oceans.

James Buchanan wanted the Oregon matter settled and he felt that it could be settled peaceably only if it were settled quickly. So in correspondence with the American minister in London he made this view clear, and began planning the steps that must be taken.

He wrote the American minister that the British must now make a proposal, and he suggested the 49th parallel proposal. He said that President Polk could then put this before Congress. Polk could not accept it outright because of the public statements that had been made on the subject. Buchanan warned that the British must not demand perpetual free navigation of the Columbia River as a part of the settlement. Polk would not accept the demand, and even if he did present such an idea to the Senate, Buchanan said, the Senate would not accept it either.

What Buchanan was worried about, he wrote to London, was lest the issue become a part of the political campaign of 1846 in Congress. General Lewis Cass of Michigan was quite capable of making this an issue in furtherance of his presidential aims, and he would not settle for the 49th parallel solution. So if the solution was to be reached, it should come before autumn.

Buchanan confided to Louis McLane, the American minister in London, that he had a personal reason, too, for wanting the matter settled.

I have for years been anxious to obtain a seat on the bench of the Supreme Court. This has been several times within my power; but circumstances have always prevented me from accepting the offered boon. I cannot desert the President, at the present moment, against his protestations. If the Oregon question should not be speedily settled, the vacancy must be filled; and then farewell to my wishes. . . .

Here, it seems, was the real measure of James Buchanan's ambition—the Supreme Court. By training and emotional makeup he was well-fitted for the court, for in the examination of all the legislation that had passed beneath his eyes during his years as congressman and senator he had never failed to test the proposed laws against the Constitution. Many other men approached legislation with an eye to achieving what they wanted or meeting what they considered to be the popular will, and then finding a constitutional prop against which to lean the law. Not Buchanan. He was a strict constructionist; that is, he always sought to find the intent of the men who had drawn up the Consitution, and he recalled forever the conditions of the various states when the Constitution was accepted and the Union was forged.

Buchanan hoped that once the Oregon issue was settled he might approach the President regarding relief from the onerous duties of Secretary of State.

In June of 1846 it was decided. President Polk was so much concerned with the Mexican problem that he did not want to waste his energies on a dispute with Britain. Yet he could not, at this time, accept the British offer to settle the Oregon question at the 49th parallel. Too much had happened. He informed Buchanan, who in turn, informed Britain, that the measure would have to be decided by the Senate. Finally, on June 12, the Senate accepted the British proposal, and with relief the administration was able to turn to other affairs.

Buchanan now did try to secure the post as Supreme Court Justice, and many men influential in government helped him for reasons of their own. Some wanted him on the bench so he would be out of the cabinet and another man might have that post. Some wanted him on the bench so he would be out of the running for the presidential nomination in 1848. A few wanted him on the bench because they thought he would make a fine judge. That was the least of the considerations, apparently.

James Buchanan (1791-1868), fifteenth President of the United States

Photograph of Harriet Lane, President Buchanan's niece, who acted as official White House hostess during the President's term

Buchanan leaving his country home, Wheatland, for Washington

President Buchanan reading his inaugural address as he begins his presidential term, 1857

President Buchanan's cabinet. Standing, left to right: Lewis Cass (Sec. of State), President Buchanan, Howell Cobb (Sec. of the Treasury), Joseph Holt (Postmaster-General). Seated, left to right: Jacob Thompson (Sec. of Interior), John B. Floyd (Sec. of War), Isaac Toucey (Sec. of the Navy), Jeremiah Black (Attorney-General)

Abolitionist John Brown's attempt to seize the arsenal at Harper's Ferry, West Virginia, 1859. In 1856 Brown led the Pottawatomie Massacre in Kansas against pro-slavery settlers.

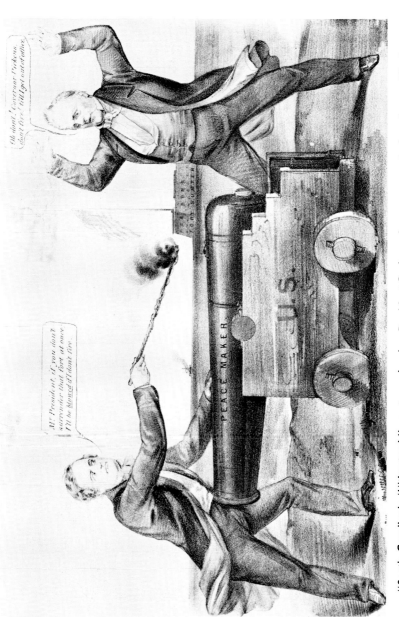

"South Carolina's 'Ultimatum'": cartoon showing President Buchanan's appeasement of southern militants

Dred Scott (1795-1858), American Negro slave who lost his suit for freedom in 1857. The Dred Scott case set the precedent that slaves were private property, and that the government had no right to interfere with or deprive a man of that property.

In the end, he lost the opportunity created by the death of Mr. Justice Baldwin because President Polk said he could not spare Buchanan from the post of Secretary of State at that time.

Indeed, President Polk did need near him a skilled and experienced diplomatist, which Buchanan most certainly was, because international questions of the day were extremely complex and pressing.

Britain and France were hopeful in 1845 and 1846 that they might persuade the Texans against annexation to the United States, and their agents in Texas worked to this end.

The British agent in Texas, Captain Elliott, combined his efforts with those of the French agent, M. Saligny, and they made representations to the people of Texas, to the effect that Britain and France would protect the Republic's independence against all comers if the Texans would reject annexation to the United States. Through Major Donaldson, his agent in Texas, Secretary Buchanan was well aware of all that the British and French were doing to prevent annexation. While worrying over the Oregon question, he still had to spend an equal amount of time and effort on the Texas problem.

The intrigue began in May, 1845, when the representatives of France and England persuaded the Texas government to sign a preliminary treaty with Mexico, which guaranteed Texas independence if she would not join the United States. The treaty was accomplished by Elliott and Saligny, who took several Texas officials to Mexico City to work out the details.

When the news came out, Texans were furious, and they were more determined than ever to go ahead with annexation when they discovered that the United States Congress went into special session in June to act on the annexation.

A special session of the Texas Congress voted for annexation in June, and a convention was held at Austin on the
Fourth of July to accept the terms of annexation.

Once this was done, an exhausted Buchanan decided to
go home to Lancaster for a rest. Two weeks later, he was
recalled to Washington by President Polk with the news
that a Mexican army of some 8,000 men had moved to the
western borders of Texas. So delicate was the problem, and
so concerned lest he arouse the nation was President Polk,
that he sent the letter to Buchanan in a plain envelope,
not using his presidential frank as he nearly always did, so
no one would know that Buchanan was returning to Washington earlier than he planned.

Buchanan returned to Washington with a plan which he
hoped would avoid war with Mexico. He wanted to reestab-
lish the diplomatic relations with Mexico, which had been
broken off in the heat of argument over the Texas annexation. He chose John Slidell of Louisiana to become a secret
representative in Mexico. Slidell's task was to arrange for
the purchase of upper California and New Mexico, and to
adjust the boundary along the north to the satisfaction of
both sides. The American government was ready to pay
as much as $40,000,000 for these lands.

John Slidell arrived in Mexico in December, 1845, and
began his efforts to prevent war. He hoped to be able to
work out a treaty, and the United States even agreed to pay
certain claims of American citizens against Mexico if the
treaty could be completed. But, in January, Slidell reported
that General Mariano Paredes had seized power in Mexico
as head of a *junta,* or temporary council, of important officials, rich hacienda owners, and army officers.

Slidell hoped to make peace, and this was Buchanan's desire, too, but events moved too rapidly for the peacemakers.
With the movement of Mexican troops north, President

Polk sent General Zachary Taylor to the border with American troops. General Paredes refused to see Slidell, although the latter carried letters from Buchanan, and Slidell then went back to New Orleans to await instructions. But it was too late, and by May, 1846, the war was begun when Mexican troops along the Nueces River attacked and captured a group of General Taylor's soldiers.

War having come, much of the initiative was taken from Secretary of State Buchanan's hands and placed in those of the military. But Buchanan kept Slidell in action at New Orleans, reporting and working, and the diplomatic side of the war was well-cared for during the next few months.

Another problem, or a part of the same that had shown itself in the Texas question, arose during the Polk administration when James Buchanan was Secretary of State. This was the growing encroachment of European nations, particularly Great Britain, on the feeble countries of South and Central America, which had so recently rebelled against Spain.

In 1845 the State Department learned of, or suspected, a British plan to take control of the Mexican province of California by first colonizing the area with British residents. Prompted by Buchanan, in his first annual message, President Polk reasserted the Monroe Doctrine of non-interference in other nations' problems, with the concurrent understanding that European nations would not interfere in the Western Hemisphere. He made it quite clear that the United States would not tolerate the creation of any new European colony on the North American continent. (On Buchanan's advice the declaration stipulated North America so that British would understand without question what was under discussion.) The ploy worked, and Britain immediately stopped what had seemed to be intensive efforts to colonize the area of California.

Britain did not give up her hopes for further influence in the Americas, however. While the United States was occupied with the Mexican War, the British moved in on Central America, where they established a protectorate over the Mosquito Indians, who lived along the Central American coast in the Guatemala-Nicaragua region. To counteract British interference, Buchanan recommended that a diplomatic representative of the United States be sent to the region. Thus, in 1847, President Polk asked Congress to appropriate money to send a *chargé d'affaires* to Guatemala, the most advanced of the Central American republics.

Then matters began to move very quickly. The Indians, whom Buchanan believed were incited by the British, began to make war on the people and government of the Yucatan Peninsula. The problem became so severe that the people of Yucatan offered to give the country to the United States in exchange for protection against the Indians. They said that if the United States did not accept the offer, it would be made to Britain and to France.

The United States did not want to take possession of this territory, but Buchanan and President Polk were unalterably opposed to giving any European power a foothold in Central America. Buchanan and President Polk conferred, and the President then recommended to Congress that aid be given the people of Yucatan, without reference to the offer of annexation. He also made it quite clear that the United States would not stand for the coming of any foreign powers into the area.

Secretary of State Buchanan then began planning a long-range policy for that area. The new *chargé d'affaires* in Guatemala was instructed to try to bring about a federation of the states of Central America.

Actually, such a federation had once existed. Just after the break with Spain, the states of Guatemala, Honduras,

Nicaragua, San Salvador, and Costa Rica had joined in an attempt to create a nation modeled on the American confederation. Their constitution was not binding, however, and soon the states fell apart, which made them prey to the ambitious Europeans. James Buchanan wanted his envoy to persuade these five nations that their future lay in union.

Britain at this time was making large and worrisome claims in behalf of her protectorate over the Mosquito Indians. She claimed that the Mosquitos had sovereignty over the Caribbean from Cape Honduras to Escuda de Veragua, which meant a good share of Honduras' coast line and all of that of Nicaragua and Costa Rica.

Buchanan sent his envoy to Central America to persuade and to listen and watch. The *chargé* was to discover just what the British were doing and planning in this region and to inform the State Department without delay. Unfortunately the *chargé* fell ill and was delayed in his trip, and in February, 1848, the British moved: they seized the port of San Juan in Nicaragua and began to increase their power in all of Central America. Soon, then, came the presidential election of 1848, and when the Whig candidate, General Zachary Taylor, was elected, the Polk administration became a caretaker administration which would hold over for more than three months after the election. Under those conditions, neither President Polk nor Secretary of State Buchanan felt it proper to begin an entirely new line of foreign policy, which would have to be assumed or rejected by their successors. The matter of Central America was left for a later day, for President Taylor to manage, and James Buchanan and the other members of the administration prepared to retire to private life.

CHAPTER 6

Politics and Statesmanship

IN THE SPRING of 1848, as he prepared to return to Pennsylvania in the knowledge that President Polk would not seek another term and so his tenure as Secretary of State would surely end the following March, James Buchanan looked around for a more gracious house than the one he occupied in the center of Lancaster. He wanted a house and a few acres of land with which to occupy himself.

He found the house and land in a small estate called Wheatland, the summer home of a Philadelphian, William Meredith, who would become Secretary of the Treasury in the cabinet of Zachary Taylor.

It was a red brick house, located a mile and a half west of the town, standing back a hundred feet from the road, screened from the road by locust and evergreen trees, and surrounded by a white fence. The house stood three stories in the wings, with two stories and an attic in the main part of the building. There was a small stable and a barn for domestic animals. It was not very large, but Buchanan did not want a large establishment. He had no use for grandeur, and, as a bachelor, he could not occupy more than one room at a time.

On retirement from the State Department, James Buchanan settled down to the life of a country squire. He was

nearly sixty years old, white-haired and tall, a very imposing, dignified man. Even in the cabinet his fellows had
called him "the squire" behind his back because of his dignity and air of authority. Mrs. Sarah Myton Maury, an English writer who lived for a time in Washington and came to
know him rather well, once described Buchanan:

"He looks like an English nobleman of thirty or forty
years ago when the grave and dignified bearing of men in
power was regarded as an essential attribute of their office,"
she wrote. But this aristocratic manner in Buchanan was
natural, she said, acquired through the habit of command,
partly, but showing Buchanan's even temper and good
character.

Mrs. Maury had seen Buchanan many times in many circumstances, and she said she could never recall the slightest
departure from his perfect self-possession. He was graceful
and good-tempered. His face was pleasantly lined, not
marked by the ravages of dissipation, and his complexion
was good. His eyes were light blue and his hands were long
and slender. He was a listener at most conversations, rather
than a speaker, but he always was abreast of the conversation and many times ahead of it in his thoughts, she said.

Nathaniel Hawthorne observed Buchanan with the eye
of a novelist and wrote that the most striking thing about
him was "a lack of polish, a kind of rusticity, notwithstanding which you feel him to be a man of the world."

He had many friends, and some very close ones, including
Senator Rufus King of Alabama, with whom he was so in-
timate that during those years in Washington they were
called "the Siamese twins."

So Buchanan settled down in the spring of 1849 to become in fact the country squire. He brought his library to
Wheatland and moved into the house. He entertained his
friends and neighbors and carried on a large correspon-

dence with political acquaintances and friends. His niece, Harriet Lane, lived with him for a time, as did two nephews. The days were spent in work in the library, and the evenings in family discussions and dinner parties. Once in a while he traveled, largely around Pennsylvania, keeping up his political connections and keeping himself in the public eye as one of the leaders of the Democratic party, which was temporarily in eclipse in Washington. He traveled to fairs and to political meetings all over the state of Pennsylvania. He visited Washington occasionally and, when he did, he wrote his niece he saw very little of the fashionable society. His time was almost constantly occupied with the politicians. Wherever he traveled, he went to church on Sunday, and he counseled his niece, now his closest relative, always to maintain her religion, and never to marry a man who had none, or who was unable to support her properly.

He was in touch with many political leaders from many parts of the nation. Virginia Democrats, knowing his feelings about the Constitution and slavery, asked him to address the Central Southern Rights Association of Virginia and to talk with them about the best means of maintaining the "Constitution and the Union of these states in their original purity"—by which they meant the rights of states, especially the right of each state to choose its own social system.

He replied that the answer was to return to the old Virginia platform of states' rights—that the powers conferred on the general government must be construed strictly, and Congress must refuse to legislate except where its power to legislate was very clear.

Buchanan found it easy to adopt this position because he had a fixed idea about the Constitution. Other men, particularly in the North, regarded the Constitution as a document made by men, thus imperfect and subject to constant adjustment. Buchanan saw the Constitution in other terms. As he wrote to some Virginia Democrats:

> . . . I consider it, to employ the expressive language of the day, as a "finality"—a fixed fact—a most important enactment of law, the agitation or disturbance of which could do no possible good, but might produce much positive evil.

Inevitably, James Buchanan would begin thinking of seeking the Presidency if for no other reason than that many southerners would push him toward it, seeing him as a northern man of reason, from their point of view. But there were many other reasons for Buchanan to think of the possibility of occupying the first executive's chair. He had been close to Presidents before, in the persons of Jackson and particularly Polk. He had served government in so many ways that he understood every facet of it. He was expert politician enough to know how to guide legislation through Congress and how to stop legislation from being enacted. In his late fifties and early sixties he was vigorous, and he still considered himself in the best of health. His moderate habits had enabled him to escape various attacks of cholera and other serious diseases that swept across the American countryside. The presidential fever came to Buchanan slowly and in such a way that it seemed most natural. It began during the Polk administration. Before that time Buchanan had never really wanted the Presidency or considered seeking it for any reason. He really wanted a seat on the Supreme Court.

Frustrated in his ambition to become a judge, Buchanan then changed course, and as he sat quietly in his library in the big house near Lancaster, he was impressed by the need for men in public life who shared a deep respect for the conservative approach to the Constitution. One cannot say that Buchanan was swallowed by ambition; much stronger than

that was his earnest belief that the Union could be pre-
served only by adopting the southern viewpoint toward the
Constitution.

By 1850 James Buchanan was indeed a candidate for the
presidential nomination of 1852, and in the spring of election year before the convention was held in Baltimore many
believed that he would receive the nomination, although
Stephen A. Douglas, the senator from Illinois, and Lewis
Cass of Michigan were very much in the running.

Buchanan's age and conservatism were liabilities, however. During the 1840's there had begun in the United
States, quite irrespective of the slavery issue, a movement
called "Young America." This movement appealed to many
Americans, for it was identified with aggressive nationalism,
free trade, and sympathy with foreign revolutions such as
that of Louis Kossuth in Hungary and the revolution in
Germany. Buchanan had been the counselor of moderation
in the Polk cabinet and he was looked upon disdainfully by
the Young Americans, who favored Stephen Douglas. But
there emerged another candidate at the convention who was
youthful and embodied many of the ideas of the Young
America group. This candidate was General Franklin
Pierce, who had served under General Winfield Scott in
the war against Mexico. The fact that he was a general was
important because the nation was greatly concerned with
military matters, and the Mexican War had not been forgotten. The previous election had brought another general
to the White House— Zachary Taylor, the hero of the Mexican War. After Taylor's death, Vice-President Millard Fillmore became President, and the administration assumed
a non-military aspect that was distinctly misleading in the
evaluation of the public sentiment of the time. When the
campaign of 1852 came around, politicians of both the
Whig and Democratic groups sensed that the voters wanted

generals again, and so Pierce became the Democratic general, and General Winfield Scott, the Whigs candidate.

Pierce did not win the nomination easily. Buchanan's friends and the supporters of Cass and Douglas did not give up quickly, and the matter was not settled until the forty-ninth ballot. As was usual when the balloting went on so long, some of the enthusiasm of the party for the candidate was lost, but in this year it did not make much difference because the Whigs were in the same position: Scott won nomination only on the fifty-third ballot at the Whig convention in Baltimore, two weeks after the Democrats had met there.

Buchanan's name was mentioned for the Vice-Presidency, but he made it quite clear in a letter from his home at Wheatland that he would not be considered for the second post. If he were nominated, he said, he would certainly decline. With the failure of his nomination in the first of the convention, he had become quite resigned to the selection of another man. He was certain that his political career was over, and said that he would never hold another political office. Part of this was pique, of course, for he was very disappointed not to have received the party's nomination.

In the beginning of the campaign of 1852 Buchanan expressed some fear that Pierce would not carry Pennsylvania. This again was a sign of his disappointment, for he asserted that he would certainly have carried the state easily had he been nominated. But Buchanan was too loyal a Democrat to sulk for long. Within a week he had convinced himself that the Pierce nomination was excellent, and he began to persuade others. He spoke for Pierce and against the Whigs, most notably at Greensburgh, Pennsylvania, in October. This speech was widely reprinted throughout Pennsylvania and other states.

After Franklin Pierce won election, much pressure was

brought on him to appoint Buchanan again as Secretary of
State to undo much of what had been done in foreign affairs
during the Whig administrations of Taylor and Fillmore.
Pierce sidestepped this pressure by saying that he ruled out
of bounds any members of former cabinets. Buchanan was
not annoyed—he could not be—because Pierce came to him
for advice on appointments, treating him as an elder statesman. Buchanan gave the advice and noted that what he
wanted to do now was to retire as gracefully as possible
to private life and devote his last years to preparation of a
book on the Polk administration, of which he had been so
vital a part.

New York's William L. Marcy was chosen as Secretary
of State in the Pierce cabinet, but, toward the end of March,
1853, the new President asked Buchanan to become Minister to England, which, aside from the cabinet posts, was
the most important job the new administration could offer.

Buchanan called at the White House and dined with the
President. Buchanan had been chosen by unanimous consent of the cabinet, President Pierce said, and not because
the post would be an honor, but because several important
issues had arisen between the United States and England,
and all cabinet members believed Buchanan was the man
most capable of settling them.

The wise old Pennsylvania politician saw several problems. First, what would Secretary Marcy think of the matter? In the first place, it was customary for the Secretary of
State and President, or at least it had been in Polk's day, to
settle such problems in Washington, not in London. Did
not Pierce want to seek settlement of differences under his
own eyes and those of Secretary Marcy?

President Pierce replied that he was certain better terms
could be achieved by working in London rather than in
Washington. As to Secretary Marcy's possible objections,

the President promised to talk to the Secretary of State to see how Marcy really felt about the appointment.

Buchanan also raised the problem of patronage. He had made several recommendations to President Pierce about appointments in Pennsylvania, he said, but the President had not followed one of them. If Buchanan were now to accept the highest possible appointment, the Pennsylvania Democrats would feel that he had sold them out in his own behalf. Pierce promised that he would make it plain to the people of Pennsylvania that no one would be denied an appointment in that state because of Buchanan's acceptance of the English mission. This was to be regarded as an appointment in behalf of the nation at large, Pierce said.

Buchanan accepted the mission, but he said he would not stay out of the country for more than two years. Still the matter was not quite settled; Buchanan's appointment had not been confirmed by the Senate.

In earlier times confirmation might not have seemed too important, but with the refusal of the Senate to confirm Martin Van Buren as Minister to England in 1831 the matter had become very important indeed. The Senate was supposed to recess on April 11, the President having told the clerk that he had no further legislation to recommend. When Buchanan heard of this, he acted. He went to see his friend Jefferson Davis, the Secretary of War, and said he guessed that the President had decided against trying to transfer the important negotiations with England from Washington to London. Davis replied that he did not think this was the case. Buchanan felt that it would be most difficult to go to England as half a minister, and he would be only half a minister until the Senate confirmed the appointment.

Davis saw Buchanan's point immediately. The next day Buchanan called at the White House and conferred again with the President. He was not pleased with the turn of events, and from the meeting came the decision that if the President could summon a quorum on Capitol Hill and secure confirmation of Buchanan, he would go to England. Otherwise the matter was ended, then and there. Fortunately, enough members of the Senate were found still to be in Washington to make a quorum, and the nomination was confirmed.

Buchanan went home to Pennsylvania for a few days to put his affairs in order, intending to return to Washington to acquaint himself with his mission, and then to leave for England toward the end of June.

Buchanan became much upset, on his return to Pennsylvania, to learn that when Pennsylvania Democrats were seeking patronage from the administration they were told that because of Buchanan's appointment the jobs must be filled elsewhere. Soon, Buchanan was convinced that President Pierce was playing a double game, intent already upon political action to secure his renomination in 1856.

Buchanan was a wily political fox. He did not break with the President or show emotion as he might have done. He went back to Washington and pretended that he was finished with politics. He attended a dinner one night at Brown's Hotel, in the company of Secretary of State Marcy, Secretary of War Davis, Attorney-General Cushing, and other influential Democratic leaders. Jefferson Davis began talking about the next election. Buchanan arose and said he wanted to make a speech. There was much good-natured joking, but the politicians did want to hear this speech from a man who was definitely a contender for the Presidency.

Buchanan stood up and said he thought that he and Secretary Marcy ought to be out of the running for the Presidency. President Pierce was a young man, and if the administration did a good job, he ought to be renominated by the

Democratic party, Buchanan said (not meaning a word of it). Secretary Marcy, whose desire for the Presidency perhaps even surpassed Buchanan's, had to follow this lead with good grace. Soon, the report of Buchanan's impromptu "speech" was all over Washington. President Pierce was lulled into believing that James Buchanan was not a threat to his political future.

Buchanan then began to occupy himself with the job at hand. As a former Secretary of State, he found the State Department to be in lamentable condition. He complained of other faults he found in the administration too, but this was not confided to others; he made notes only for his diary.

Before he left Washington, Buchanan saw that he had three major problems to resolve with the British. The first was the question of reciprocal trade between the two nations and the adjustment of tariffs; second, was the problem of fisheries, on the Atlantic coast in particular; third, was the explosive situation that existed in Latin America, which had not really been solved by the Clayton-Bulwer Treaty made during the previous administration, although that treaty seemed to deal with the issues between the two countries. Buchanan hoped to use the British desire to establish good trade relations as a lever to force the British to abandon their foothold in the Central American region where they were so unwelcome to the Americans, but he was not at all sure this was possible, pointing out to friends that the British had never voluntarily abandoned a commercial position once it was established. Yet, he was certain that if agreement could not be reached there would eventually be war between the United States and Britain over Central America.

In mid-June Buchanan was not at all sure that he was going to England. President Pierce kept telling him he wanted the situation to be discussed in London, but Buchanan kept believing that the President was not totally frank with him, and he probed to see if he would have the powers necessary to carry out his mission. Without them, to go to England would be political suicide and would lead to diplomatic failure.

He wrote to Pierce, asking for reassurance and phrasing his letter in such a way that the President might easily rescind the appointment. There was no answer, so on June 23 he wrote again, this time indicating that he wished to be relieved of the appointment because the President had obviously changed his mind. It was only two weeks before his expected sailing day.

Within a few days he had a reply. If President Pierce had been vacillating, he had now made up his mind to go ahead. The President said that he had mislaid the letter, and he apologized profusely. So it was settled, or it seemed to be. But Buchanan wanted assurances that he would be called upon to settle the matters before the State Department, and at that time he knew that Secretary Marcy was discussing some of them with the British diplomats in Washington. The matter dragged on; Buchanan demanded either to be relieved of the mission or given power; and Pierce continued to press him to take the mission, but did not grant the power.

The original sailing day came and went. On July 11, President Pierce went to Philadelphia on a visit, and Buchanan traveled there to talk to him. He had decided to reject the mission if he could do so without an open break with Pierce. He knew now, and so did the newspapers, that the fishery question was under discussion in Washington, and he felt strongly that unless all outstanding difficulties could be put into one package, there was no chance of pushing the British out of the new colony they had established in Central America.

It was a difficult time for everyone. The President was busy receiving the homage of the notables of the region. Buchanan saw him at a reception, and then the next day he visited Pierce at McKibbins' Hotel and rode with him aboard a steamboat to Camden, across the Delaware. They talked as they rode, but they were interrupted almost constantly.

President Pierce said again that he wanted Buchanan to take the mission, and he hoped that it would not be declined at this late date. At this particular time there was considerable danger that the fisheries problem would bring about some uncomfortable moments. Britain had recently sent a fleet of warships to the fishing banks of the Atlantic to enforce her views of the fishing treaty then in effect.

Buchanan had come to believe that Secretary Marcy and President Pierce were playing a double game. It seemed that ever since they had offered him the mission to London they had been trying to settle the questions, piecemeal, in Washington. Buchanan was still strong in his belief that all the questions between the United States and England must be settled simultaneously. Only thus, he said—and he said it time and time again in person and in letters—would the American position be strong enough against mighty Great Britain so that an envoy in London could emerge from the negotiations with honor.

Among other things, Buchanan obviously was acutely conscious of his own position and what might be done to it by a diplomatic failure in London, which could be laid at his door.

But now, on this trip across the Delaware River, it became clear to Buchanan that he could not decline the mission to London without creating an open breach with the administration. Such a breach would turn many Democrats against him and work against any chances he might have of achieving the presidential nomination in 1856. It was agreed before the steamboat reached Camden. There, Buchanan took his leave of the President and his party, who went on to New York, and returned to Wheatland to prepare for his departure.

Before he left the United States, James Buchanan went to some trouble to secure all the documents and papers relative to the dispute in Central America. President Pierce had expressed some surprise when Buchanan said he did not have them. The reason might have been some attempt by Secretary Marcy to make life difficult for a rival, but it was more likely the confused situation in the Department of State in those days. No matter how high his qualifications as a statesman, Daniel Webster, who had been first Secretary of State in the Fillmore cabinet, had not been much of a bureaucratic housekeeper. When he left office after two years, the State Department was in confusion as far as papers and procedures went. Edward Everett, Webster's successor, was not a great deal better in this regard, and Marcy, who had considerable experience in administration as a governor, still had not yet learned the niceties of the handling of foreign affairs.

Finally, in August, James Buchanan had secured what he wanted, and cheerfully and firmly he went aboard the steamship "Atlantic" for the voyage to Liverpool, a passage of about ten days' duration.

In the beginning, Buchanan lived in a hotel in London, where he was horrified at having to pay $90 a week for a suite of three rooms. "The enormous expenses here," he wrote to his niece, "and the superior attractions there drive all the American visitors to Paris and the continent." He also complained about the number of tourists who stopped through London, saying that he spent much of his time issuing passports.

Shortly after his arrival in London, Minister Buchanan was involved in a controversy which was no fault of his own. Secretary of State Marcy had for some time been bothered by the requests of some diplomats for uniform allowances or by their complaints about the cost of outfitting themselves to appear at the various courts of the world. The diplomatic corps wore splendid uniforms of gold braid and heavy materials so that they would not be mistaken for palace servants, who wore ordinary full-dress suits at court sessions. Marcy found the idea of uniforms quite unpalatable to many Americans because it smacked of the idolotry of kings and queens. He issued a directive in the fall of 1853 to all embassies and legations to the effect that the heads of American delegations should always appear at the courts "in the simple dress of an American citizen." Buchanan discussed this matter with Major General Sir Edward Cust, the master of ceremonies of the English court, when the two met one day at the Travellers Club in London. The General became quite red in the face as he considered the prospects.

He told Minister Buchanan that it would be improper for him to appear at court in simple formal dress. He would look like one of the butlers, the General said, and the Queen would be insulted.

Buchanan asked what he could do. His government had spoken, and he was bound to obey the wishes of the Secretary of State. He said, hopefully, that if the Queen suggested that he appear in costume he would feel it was necessary to comply with her wishes. The General said the Queen would receive him in any costume he wore, but she would not like it if he did not conform to the rules of the court. Further, he said, the people of England would not like it.

Buchanan pointed out that Senator Stephen A. Douglas had just returned from St. Petersburg, the most formal court in the world, and that Douglas had appeared before the Czar wearing ordinary dress. Count Nesselrode had asked what dress the Senator wore when he appeared before the President of the United States and said he was willing to accept Douglas in that attire. Buchanan also noted that when he had lived in Russia as minister he had dressed simply, without arousing animosity.

At the end of this discussion it appeared likely to Minister Buchanan that he would be placed "socially in Coventry" on this question of dress—that he would not be invited to court or to the balls of lesser royalty and the Queen's other courtiers.

This made no difference personally, Buchanan told Secretary Marcy in a letter, but it might keep him from making a success of his mission.

So the problem was presented. It continued.

In February, 1854, the Queen opened Parliament. Since this was a ceremonial occasion, all the foreign diplomats were expected to be present. General Sir Edward Cust sent a printed circular around to every foreign mission in London, noting the opening of Parliament and requesting the presence of the ministers. "No one can be admitted into the Diplomatic Tribune, or in the body of the House, but in full court dress," said the circular.

Thereupon, Minister Buchanan decided that he would not embarrass himself or the Queen. He would not attend the opening of Parliament.

So the ceremony was held, without the presence of the American minister in London, and the newspapers asked openly why Mr. Buchanan was not there. The suggestion was made that this was an open insult from the American government to the British crown.

General Sir Edward was upset, and so was Buchanan. The entire court was stirred by the problem.

It was resolved in very short order, however, when the Queen held her first levée, or morning reception, of the season. Minister Buchanan announced that he would present himself at court in his usual dress, but wearing a plain dress sword. And so he did appear, wearing a black coat, white vest and cravat, black pantaloons and dress boots, and a black-handled, black-hilted dress sword. The sword distinguished him as a gentleman, and no more was heard. The Queen was pleased that the American minister honored her with an open mark of respect, and what had come near to being a diplomatic scandal became a minor triumph for Buchanan.

As for his mission, Buchanan faced serious difficulties. Lord Palmerston, the Prime Minister, was committed to the spread of British colonialism, not to its retrenchment anywhere. Two years after Buchanan's arrival in London, the matter was still not settled, nor did it seem much closer to settlement than it had on the day that he set out for England. Britain was occupied with the Crimean War; and at home the worry was largely domestic—over slavery and the admission of Kansas to the Union. In the Kansas Territory the pro-slavery forces were in control of the legislature, but anti-slavery men were carrying out raids and terrorizing much of the countryside. In this heightened atmosphere of tension, the problems of Central America and British-American relations did not seem nearly so momentous as they had in 1853.

Consequently, although Buchanan's correspondence and meetings with the British on the construction of the Clayton-Bulwer treaty did not ever come to mean a change in the treaty, as had originally been expected, the pressure was no longer apparent. Britain slackened her expansionism in the west because she was busy at war with Russia. Minister Buchanan could do no more than he had done, and he certainly had not failed.

In the spring of 1856 Buchanan announced his intention of retiring from the post and asked that another minister to Britain be found. The appointment was some time in coming, but it was made in February, and Buchanan was free to return to the United States.

During Buchanan's absence, the atmosphere of his own country had changed markedly. Until midway in the Pierce administration, the question of slavery seemed to be as knotty and impossible as ever, but no more so than it had been four or eight or twelve years earlier. But in 1854, after Kansas was opened for settlement, the struggle concentrated there, and the formula for "popular sovereignty" was tested. This meant that the people who settled the territory should decide how it would come into the Union, as a free state or as a slave state. Left alone, left to normal settlement procedures, this plan might have been satisfactory. But from the North came organized groups of settlers whose purpose was not so much to seek new lands for themselves as to be sure that Kansas and Nebraska territories would be settled as free states. When that became known in the South, the southerners sent their own groups to the western territories. For the first time, the question of settlement was not nearly as important as the question of what kind of settlement. The winds of war were beginning to blow.

In London, even, it was possible to feel these winds and to know how serious was the problem developing in America. James Buchanan sensed the change. He wrote to William Marcy about the coming four years:

> I believe that the next presidential term will perhaps be the most important and responsible of any which has occurred since the origin of the government, and whilst no competent and patriotic man to whom it may be offered should shrink from the responsibility, yet he may well accept it as the greatest trial of his life.

And there was no question about it now, James Buchanan was seeking that trial and the presidential post for 1856.

CHAPTER 7

The Campaign of 1856

WHEN JAMES BUCHANAN ARRIVED in New York toward the end of April, 1856, he discovered, to no one's surprise, that he was a prime candidate for the Democratic nomination for the Presidency. Why should he not be? Among those who worried over the fate of the country, he was agreed to be an ideal candidate; for he lived in the industrial North, yet his sympathies were with the South. The abolitionists could not find fault with his personal conduct, for he avowed his hatred of slavery and avowed it often, but for so many years he had repeated his position on the constitutionality of slavery, based on ancient rights, that the South believed him when he said he would never condone action that would destroy the rights of southerners to hold slaves as property.

By June, Buchanan had been nominated by the Democratic convention of the state of Pennsylvania (it had been declared unanimous at the end), and his friends in North and South were working hard for him.

The first week in June arrived, and with it the Democratic national convention, which was this year held in Cincinnati. The three candidates for the nomination were President Pierce, Senator Douglas, and James Buchanan. One of Buchanan's friends, S. M. Barlow of New York City, decided he would do all in his power to achieve the nomination of the Pennsylvanian, so he took a house in Cincinnati and invited known supporters of Buchanan to stay there during the meeting. A number accepted, including John Slidell of Louisiana, who had been working hard for Buchanan in the South.

Before the convention began, Buchanan's friends congregated and discussed the dangers to their candidate. Foremost of the dangers was the "Soft" delegation of New York State, which was pledged to support Stephen Douglas. (Hard and Soft in this case did not represent views on slavery but concerned internal New York State politics.) If the "Hards" could be seated, then support of Buchanan would be assured from the important state of New York.

Senator James A. Bayard of Delaware, one of Buchanan's friends, secured appointment as chairman of the credentials committee, and as such he heard the arguments of the two competing New York delegations. The majority of the committee consisted of Douglas men, and they voted to seat the Softs. Senator Bayard and the rest of the minority held that the convention ought to seat half of each New York delegation, and when the committee report was presented to the entire convention for adoption Bayard was so persuasive that he convinced the majority of the convention to do just this. So, in a long session, the Buchanan men won the first battle of the convention.

On the first ballot, Buchanan polled 135 votes, President Pierce polled 122, and Senator Douglas had only 33 votes. By the tenth ballot, Pierce was finished, Buchanan had 168, and Douglas, 121. This meant Buchanan had a majority of votes, but he did not have the required two-thirds. Soon he would have, however, and Douglas could see that, so he moved to have Buchanan nominated without further balloting. Thus, Buchanan was nominated unanimously on the next ballot.

For the first time, an organization that called itself the Republican party emerged to hold a convention this year. For the first time also, an important segment of the political men of the country found in that party an area of agreement on the matter of slavery. They adopted a platform which included a statement of absolute opposition to slavery in the territories and the immediate admission of Kansas as a free state.

Thus, in 1856, for the first time in American history, the question of slavery was openly before the American people as a political issue. Those who wanted slavery eliminated saw that their support belonged to the Republican party, which had nominated John C. Fremont. Those who supported slavery then, were pushed away from the Republican party (although it still had much the makeup of the old Whig party) and pushed toward either the Democratic party or the American party, which nominated Millard Fillmore, the former President. Most, by far, tended to move to the Democratic party. Within that party were many moderates and men who had no use for slavery. There were also the strict Constitutionalists, such as James Buchanan. Indeed, a man had to be either a strict Constitutionalist or a slavery advocate to accept the fellowship of the southerners.

As was the custom, the presidential nominees made a great show of not having sought the nation's highest office, and when they were chosen, they made a show of not campaigning. Nevertheless, they did campaign, making sure that their supporters made speeches in the proper places at the proper time. Pennsylvania was a vital point in the campaign of 1856; popular as Buchanan was there and well

known as he was in the state, it would be no easy matter
to carry Pennsylvania. That spring, before the Democratic
convention, when the issue of Kansas was being debated
heatedly in Congress, Senator Charles Sumner of Massachusetts had arisen and spoken strongly about the "rape"
of Kansas by the southerners, who had taken control of
the territorial legislature and sought admission of Kansas
as a slave state. Sumner was strong, and some said he was
coarse and vulgar, in his denunciation of several individuals, including Senator Andrew P. Butler of South
Carolina. A few days later, Butler's nephew, Representative
Preston S. Brooks of South Carolina, entered the Senate
chamber and assaulted Sumner with a heavy cane, striking
him repeatedly and knocking him unconscious. Sumner
was taken to the hospital for medical treatment, and his
injuries were so severe that he did not return to the Senate
regularly until 1859, three years later.

Which was worse, Sumner's indecent verbal assault on
southern legislators who considered themselves gentlemen
or Brooks' indecent physical assault on the older senator?
Men in North and South took sides immediately, depending on how their sympathies lay. The issue gave them an
opening to vent their spleen, and there were many arguments and quarrels over the rights and wrongs of the Sumner affair. Representative Brooks resigned his seat in the
House of Representatives following harsh criticisms in
Washington—and then was overwhelmingly reelected to
the same seat by his constituents in South Carolina.

Pennsylvania borders Maryland; along the rolling country where the states meet one could scarcely note the difference between free Pennsylvania and slave Maryland off-
hand, and in southern Pennsylvania there were many who
sympathized with the South, even though they did not
hold slaves. In the northern sections of the state it was not

so. Pennsylvania was also a stronghold of the abolitionists. And so the election in Pennsylvania in 1856 occupied more than its usual importance. There were other reasons: the election of state officials came early, in October, and the results would be closely watched because the voters would show their preferences. Then, too, the Democratic candidate, James Buchanan, was a Pennsylvania man. How would that affect the state election, even though the voters in October were not casting ballots for or against him?

Many observers believed that the crisis in American politics would be reached in this election, and James Buchanan was among them. When the vote was counted and Pennsylvania's Democrats had won in the state election, Buchanan spoke to a large number of his friends and supporters who came to pay their respects at Wheatland.

"The people of the North seems to have forgotten the warning of the Father of his Country against geographical parties," he said. He regarded as most dangerous of all the party of combined North which would oppose the party of combined South on the question of slavery. This was what he and others had feared with the emergence of the new Republican party from the ashes of Whiggery.

He was confident now, he said, that the crisis was past with the Democratic victory in Pennsylvania. Then, James Buchanan summed up the position of the moderate Democrats in the year 1856:

The storm of abolition against the South has been gathering for almost a quarter of a century. It had been increasing by every various form of agitation which fanaticism could devise. We had reached the crisis. The danger was imminent. Republicanism was sweeping over the North like a tornado. It appeared to be resistless in its course. The blessed Union of these States—the last hope for human liberty on earth—appeared to be tottering on its base. Had Pennsylvania yielded, had she become an abolition state, without a special interposition of Divine Providence, we should have been precipitated into the yawning gulf of dissolution. But she stood erect and firm as her own Alleghenies. She breasted the storm and drove it back. The night is departing, and the roseate and propitious morn now breaking upon us promises a long day of peace and prosperity for our country. To secure this, all we of the North have to do is to permit our southern neighbors to manage their own domestic affairs, as they permit us to manage ours. It is merely to adopt the golden rule, and do unto them as we would they should do unto us, in the like circumstances. All they ask from us is simply to let them alone. This is the whole spirit and essence of the much abused Cincinnati platform (of the Democrats). This does no more than adopt the doctrine which is the very root of all our institutions, and to recognize the right of a majority of the people of a territory, when about to enter the Union as a state, to decide for themselves whether domestic slavery shall or shall not exist among them. This is not to favor the extension of slavery, but simply to deny the right of an abolitionist in Massachusetts or Vermont to prescribe to the people of Kansas what they shall or shall not do in regard to this question.

In 1856 an additional threat to the strength of the Democratic party came in the form of the American or Know-Nothing party, which had as its principal platform the election to all public offices of persons who were native-born Americans. The party took a strong position against Catholics (John C. Fremont was Roman Catholic), for states' rights, and for strict control of immigration. This party was a threat, having nominated former President Fillmore, but Buchanan quickly saw that his contest was with Fremont, and his supporters made it quite clear that this was true. The fight the Democrats waged in the campaign was based on the "sectionalism" of the Republican party, which represented North and West, but not the

South, and its obvious position against the states' rights theory and against slavery.

In this formative period, there were some strange political alliances. The New England Whig leader Rufus Choate wrote friends in Maine saying that the duty of the Whigs was to unite with some party to defeat the "new geographical party calling itself Republican." If the Republicans were to win an election, he said, the Union would be in danger of dissolution. He said he, a Whig, would support Buchanan.

The Pennsylvania state election victory was not as great as Buchanan and the other Democrats had hoped. The Democrats won by 3,000 votes out of a total of 423,000, but they had still won, and this fact was made known all across the country.

A month after the Pennsylvania state election came the presidential balloting. When the votes were counted, Buchanan had 1,838,169, Fremont had 1,341, 264, and Fillmore had 874,534. Buchanan was President-elect, although he had not won a majority of all the votes cast and would be a minority President. Those who looked at the election carefully could see trouble ahead because of this fact and because of the manner in which the voters had reacted to the parties. Buchanan's strength was in the South; Fremont's strength was in the North; and Fillmore's strength was also in the South, among those who feared disunion under Democratic rule.

So observers decided that what had happened in the election was that the American party had lost the election, and made certain it would go out of existence; the Democrats had won the election, but had sacrificed the strength of the Democratic party in the North; and the Republicans had lost the election, but had gained control of the North and West.

For an incoming President, the election returns were dismaying. For the first time the country was truly and openly devoted to sectionalism. In the North and West, Buchanan had won only the votes of the free states of Pennsylvania, New Jersey, Indiana, Illinois, and California. If, in 1860, the Republicans could capture the votes of these non-slave states, they could win the election.

Buchanan's problem, then, was to do what he could to heal the breach within the union of American states. Never had a President been elected with but a single serious problem before him which dominated all others, and with so clear an understanding of the nature of the problem as Buchanan had.

He, the Democratic party, and the nation would all stand or fall on the accomplishments of his administration in the coming four years.

CHAPTER 8

President

"THE GREAT OBJECT of my administration will be to arrest, if possible, the agitation of the slavery question at the North, and to destroy sectional parties." So wrote James Buchanan to a friend in December, 1856, two months after his election as President, as he considered what he must do to accomplish his aim.

One of the first things to do was to be sure that he had people around him whom he could trust absolutely. He chose as his private secretary, his nephew, James Buchanan Henry. He selected his cabinet with unusual care, choosing three men from the South, three men from the North and West, and one from Tennessee, a border state which was as torn by dissension as the Union itself. Then in February, 1857, he set out for Washington.

The Washington toward which Buchanan moved from his home in Wheatland was more upset than ever before. The results of the election raised questions about the repeal of the Compromise of 1820, known as the Missouri Compromise, and the wrecking of the Compromise of 1850. These events had occurred not long before, during the Pierce administration.

The change had been made in the Kansas-Nebraska Act of 1854, which had been introduced by Senator Stephen A.

Douglas of Illinois, chairman of the Senate committee on territories, and it was passed after the breach it caused had been made almost irreparable.

The struggle began that year, 1854, when citizens of the area which is now divided into Kansas and Nebraska began agitation for admission as a new state. Some of the people in this area were southerners and slave-owners, particularly those in the southern area of the territory. In the north, in the part we now know as Nebraska, there were very few slaveholders.

In January, 1854, Senator Douglas introduced a bill providing for the admission of a new state which would be called Nebraska. This state would comprise the land area that is now both Nebraska and Kansas.

Nebraska might have come into the Union as a free state, twice as large as it is today, had the discussion not developed political overtones. Relatively speaking, there were few slaveholders in the area, but Senator Dixon of Kentucky, a Whig, decided that he would make an issue of this matter. He proposed that when the bill came up he would move to have the Missouri Compromise outlawed.

Senator Dixon's action was prompted by two lines of thought. As a border-state southerner, he was concerned about the preservation of the balance in Congress between slave and free states. As a Whig, he was concerned about the power of the Democrats, and he sought to embarrass Senator Douglas, who was the leader of the Democrats in Congress.

Douglas was not to be so easily trapped as a politician, and so he brought up a compromise measure which indeed trapped him as a statesman. He suggested that it was time for a new congressional attitude toward the development of the various territories seeking statehood. The people, he said, should be sovereign, and by the people he meant the people who actually lived in the territory seeking statehood.

In principle, this doctrine was irreproachable. It pointed toward the highest pinnacle to which a democratic republic might rise—the sovereignty of the people, exercised in the public interest only. But, in practice, the Douglas plan left a great deal to be desired.

The Douglas proposal called for the division of the Nebraska Territory into two territories, to be called Nebraska and Kansas. There were virtually no slave-holding settlers in the northern or Nebraska section. There were a number of slave-holding settlers in the southern or Kansas section quite probably a majority. At least many in Congress believed there was a majority, and these legislators supposed that Kansas would come in as a slave state and Nebraska as a free state and thus the balance would again be maintained, and the Union might limp along a little longer without resolution of the major question facing and dividing North and South.

Senator Douglas's proposal immediately came to be known as "squatter sovereignty," an undignified term thrust upon it by cynics and the press. The word squatter referred to a new settler. Most squatters came without resources or much money in hand. They were settlers, and they were attracted by the promise of lands that could be had from the federal government by homesteading.

In early days, the word squatter had referred to illegal settlers who simply moved into lands, staked out their claims, and refused to move from them. By 1805 the intrusion of squatters into the Louisiana Territory had become so serious that two years later Congress passed a law called the Intrusion Act which authorized stiff penalties for squatters. But as the United States grew westward, it was impossible to enforce this law, and it withered away.

By 1820 a credit system for purchase of federal lands was put into effect by Congress. Settlers could buy land at $1.25 an acre, provided they bought at least 80 acres.

Senator Thomas Hart Benton fought for lands for settlers who had preempted or squatted on them, and in 1830 he secured passage of a law which established the figure of 160 acres as the standard portion of land a new settler could take on.

During the quarter of a century that followed, the principle was established that the public lands of the West belonged to those who would risk life and limb to make the sacrifices to settle the land. So, by 1854, the principle of squatter sovereignty had lost the sting that was originally in the words, and squatter meant settler.

Senator Douglas is said to have believed that the very nature of this whole territory would tend to keep both Kansas and Nebraska as non-slave regions. There was very little about Kansas and Nebraska that compared with the South. The land was flat grassland for the most part, suitable for raising stock. There were flat bottoms nestled between rolling hills; there was also dry land that reminded one more of the harsh Southwest than of the lush Black Belt.

But in the 1850's the configuration of the land was not the deciding factor in the southern settlement. The leaders of the South were fighting for preservation of their social system, and to be effective their fight must be waged in Congress. To fight they must keep their forces as equal as possible with those of the northerners.

So the South embraced the Douglas compromise as an opportunity to move in with settlers and to take control of Kansas, leaving Nebraska to the northerners.

The idea of popular sovereignty in the territories had originated with Lewis Cass, the senator from Michigan. It was accepted enthusiastically by the South and by northern and western senators who wished to avoid a fight. Not all accepted, and not all Democrats favored the idea. A group calling themselves the Independent Democrats published an appeal to Congress condemning the Kansas-Nebraska bill as a violation of the pledge of an earlier Congress that slavery would not be extended into the territory acquired from France known as the Louisiana Purchase.

They failed to make a serious impression on others in Congress. On March 3, 1854, the Senate passed the bill known as the Kansas-Nebraska Act by a vote of 37–14. On May 22, the House of Representatives passed the bill by a much smaller margin—113 votes for and 100 votes against. This vote in itself showed just what the South was worried about. The large vote against the bill represented the growing movement for abolition of slavery that was centered in the North. Only by maintenance of the South's power in the Senate, based on two seats for every state, regardless of population, could the South keep hated legislation from being enacted by a more populous and growing North. If Douglas's first plan had been accepted and Nebraska Territory had been admitted as a free state, two more senators and perhaps two more representatives would have entered Congress to support northern measures. If Kansas could be brought in as a slave state, then the ratio would remain the same.

The southerners set out in 1854 to colonize Kansas, where they already had a nucleus of sympathizers. At the same time, the Kansas-Nebraska Act became the watchword of northern Whigs, and in the flame of emotion that developed was hardened the force that would become the Republican party.

James Buchanan was in England when these events occurred. He was in England as the fighting in Kansas began, too. He was thus spared the political necessity of taking a position on the issue. To have taken a position might have put an end to his political career because in truth his position was that "in sustaining the repeal of the Missouri Compromise, the senators and representatives of the southern states became the aggressors themselves" for the first time. Buchanan had always held that the South was much put-upon by hotheads of the North. Now all he could do was hold his tongue in wonderment that the southern position had been offered by a representative of the North, Senator Douglas.

Hardly had President Pierce's ink dried on the Kansas-Nebraska Act when the fighting in Kansas began. In November, 1854, John Whitfield was elected territorial delegate to Congress. Whitfield was the candidate of the slavery men, and the election was marked by fraud, intimidation, and corruption on both sides. It was simply impossible for Congress to do what it had done—to walk away and tell the people of Kansas and Nebraska in effect to "fight the issue out among themselves"—without producing violence and bloodshed.

Thousands of armed men roamed Kansas in bands. The majority of them at this time were from Missouri and represented the slave interests. The bands so frightened the people of Kansas that in the election of the territorial legislature a heavy majority of slaveholders and pro-slavery men was elected. Governor Andrew H. Reeder of Kansas, appointed by President Pierce, was so intimidated by these armed men that he refused to declare the election fraudulent although there was no question that there had been fraud on both sides.

In July, 1855, the pro-slavery legislature met at Pawnee and enacted laws that were intended to muzzle the anti-slavery agitators.

The anti-slavery faction was not to be permanently intimidated, however, and men who called themselves Free Soilers met on September 5 to repudiate the pro-slavery legislature and to call upon Congress to admit Kansas into the Union as a free state. Arms began to pour into the state from North and South. Each side appointed a "military commander," and the two factions prepared for outright war.

By the beginning of 1856 the Free Soilers had elected their own governor and legislature. They attempted to show that they were not abolitionists by passing a law which prohibited free Negroes as well as slaves from coming into Kansas. But the southerners were not appeased, for matters had gone much too far, and the South knew that in the Kansas-Nebraska Act lay its only hope for retention of political power on the old basis.

President Pierce sent a special message to Congress toward the end of January, 1856, condemning the Topeka government, which was the Free Soil government, and indicating to those versed in politics that he was siding with the southerners.

Then came open warfare, including John Brown's Pottawatomie Massacre, in which five pro-slavery colonists living at Dutch Henry's Crossing on Pottawatomie Creek were murdered, and the sacking of Lawrence by the South, which had caused Brown to move.

Throughout the election year of 1856, the struggle over Kansas continued. The Free Soil men submitted a constitution to Congress, and the House of Representatives voted to accept Kansas as a free state. The Senate refused. The House then refused to seat either the pro-slavery or Free Soil delegate from the territory.

President Pierce was denied renomination by the Democratic party because he had become involved in this issue thus had become too controversial a figure within the party. The Democrats were sorely divided on the manner of dealing with the slavery struggle, and, consequently James Buchanan was chosen to lead the party in 1856. He was the great conciliator who had the undeniable advantage of being out of the country during the argument over Kansas.

He could not long stay out of the struggle. In Congress early in 1857 it became apparent that no agreement could be reached either on the seating of the delegates of the two sides or on the acceptance of one proposed constitution or the other. James Buchanan faced a most difficult situation. He resolved it within the framework of his conscience, quite as one would have expected. He chose to support the pro-southern territorial legislature, not because it was pro-southern, but because it had been elected as specified by Congress and had never been repudiated by Congress. The Topeka government of Free Soil men had not been authorized by anyone.

A President with a different turn of mind might have struggled to have both governments outlawed in order to resolve the problem in Kansas on the basis of congressional control of elections. But that was not Buchanan's way. He was of judicial temperament, and not executive. His strongest personal ambition had been to achieve a seat on the United States Supreme Court. It was only when he was frustrated in this design that he had cast serious eyes on the position of chief executive. Had Buchanan been offered a choice at any time between the office of Chief Justice of the Supreme Court and of President (which, of course, could never be) he would unhesitatingly have chosen the judicial post.

All that Buchanan was to do in the next four years must be measured against his own character, leanings, and the particularly specific and detailed regard for law as such, without consideration of the moral strength or weakness of that law.

James Buchanan assumed office in March, 1857. Almost immediately, he was embroiled in the Kansas question. By summer, he was under attack. Forty-three distinguished citizens of Connecticut prepared a memorial to the President, accusing him of violating his oath of office by supporting the slaveholders. He replied: ". . . I found the government of Kansas as well-established as that of any other territory." Congress had accepted the Kansas legislature, notwithstanding the dispute about the validity of the election. Buchanan wrote in his own defense:

Under these circumstances, what was my duty? Was it not to sustain this government, to protect it from the violence of lawless men, who were determined either to rule or ruin, to prevent it from being overturned by force? . . .

Would you have desired that I abandon the territorial government, sanctioned as it had been by Congress, to illegal violence and thus renew the scenes of civil war and bloodshed which every patriot in the country had deplored? This would, indeed, have been to violate my oath of office, and to fix a damning blot on the character of my administration.

In his inaugural address, President Buchanan had upheld the Douglas idea of non-interference with slavery in the states and popular sovereignty in the territories. Was he leaning to the southern position? He had always leaned thus, because of his interpretation of the Constitution and of the intentions of the founding fathers.

Was all his talk about law, then, a smokescreen to hide his basic sympathy with the South? It could not be stated so simply as that. Personally, Buchanan inclined toward the southerners because he liked their manners and their way of life. The South was far more reminiscent to him of the civilization of Europeans which he had grown to enjoy than the brusque ways of the New Englanders, the roughness of the westerners, and the preoccupation with business and industry of the people of the Atlantic states.

From the beginning of his public career, James Buchanan had shown the love of the law that marks a good lawyer. Certainly, his personality inclined toward the South, but so did his sense of justice.

Almost at the beginning of his administration, President Buchanan was forced to take action regarding Kansas. In 1856 a fellow Pennsylvanian, John W. Geary, had been appointed governor of the territory of Kansas by President Pierce, after the resignation of the second territorial governor, Wilson Shannon, who had been a pro-slavery man, and the temporary appointment of an acting governor, who was also pro-slavery. Governor Geary appeared to be pro-slavery as well. He called out federal troops to put down an insurrection by the northern roughnecks and did not seem to be much inclined to move against the southern roughnecks.

By the autumn of 1856, however, Geary's attitude had changed. He no longer supported either side, but wanted to secure justice for Kansas. He tried to follow a non-partisan course in Kansas, but President Pierce did not support Geary as strongly as the Governor thought he should, so on March 4, 1857, Geary resigned. As a result, President Buchanan was forced to act on the Kansas question.

He appointed Robert J. Walker of Mississippi as governor. "Pro-slavery," shouted the Free Soilers. But it was not as simple as that, once again, for Walker made a serious effort to secure free votes and fair treatment of both sides in Kansas. He pledged that any constitution that was adopted by a constitutional convention would be submitted to a fair vote of the people.

The Free Soil supporters listened to Walker and agreed

to participate in the election of the new legislature, although they had earlier refused to do so.

Territorial elections were held in the autumn of 1857, and Governor Walker was as good as his word. He and the territorial secretary looked closely at the balloting and threw out thousands of fraudulent votes cast by the pro-slavery men.

The final results of the Kansas territorial election of 1857 gave the Free Soil party a majority in both houses of the legislature.

Meanwhile, however, the old pro-slavery legislature had met at Lecompton in January, 1857, and ordered that a constitutional convention be held in the fall. So, just two weeks after the pro-slavery legislature was replaced by the Free Soil legislature, the convention was held, and its pro-slavery delegates drew up a state constitution which guaranteed the right of slavery in Kansas.

Coming, as it did, on the heels of a fair election which proved that most people in Kansas wanted a free state, the Lecompton Constitution aroused a wave of feeling in the North. Newspaper editors denounced it. So did ministers in their pulpits. Thousands of people in the North wrote to the President and to Congress, demanding that the Lecompton Constitution be disregarded.

Governor Walker felt the same way. He journeyed to Washington to see President Buchanan and in the privacy of the President's study he told Buchanan the facts—how he had stepped in and prevented bloodshed and the violation of the people's rights by enforcing the laws with the assistance of federal troops, and how the southerners had tried to stuff the ballot boxes. He told the President that he was absolutely certain that the majority of the people of Kansas backed the new legislature and that they wanted Kansas to be a free state.

In December, 1857, President Buchanan was faced with

the momentous decision regarding the Lecompton Constitution. Governor Walker counselled against accepting it.
Senator Stephen Douglas, who had created the monster of
popular sovereignty, also counselled against acceptance.

The Free Soil forces in Kansas sent word that they would
not vote at all when the Lecompton Constitution came up
for ratification on December 21.

On the other side, southern senators and representatives
counselled in favor of the Lecompton Constitution. They
pointed out to the President that under law the constitution was perfectly valid; it had been formed by a convention
called by the duly elected legislators of Kansas. The fact
that these legislators had been chosen in fraudulent elections was carefully avoided. The southerners pointed to the
recent election of a Free Soil legislature as proof that there
was no coercion or collusion in Kansas.

President Buchanan wavered. In the end, his cabinet
helped him decide, and in deciding he took the position,
justified by only the narrowest interpretation of law, that
the Lecompton Constitution would be valid if it was accepted. Of course, it was known that the constitution would
be accepted because only the pro-slavery men were going
to vote on it; the Free Soil supporters had announced their
boycott.

It became known in Kansas that the President was leaning toward the Lecompton Constitution, and the Free Soil
supporters decided that they must take strong action to
persuade the President and Congress that the Lecompton
Constitution could not be honored or accepted. The leaders
of the Free Soil party met with Frederick P. Stanton, the
territorial secretary (in the absence of Governor Walker,
Secretary Stanton was acting governor), and the Free Soilers persuaded Stanton to call a session of the legislature on
December 7, well in advance of the date scheduled for the
legislature to convene. The purpose was to show the nation

that the legislature of Kansas did not want a constitution permitting slavery.

Under the voting rules established by the old, pro-slavery legislature, the people were to vote on only one part of the constitution: an article that guaranteed the right of slave property. If the article was accepted by the people, Kansas would be a slave state. If it was rejected by the people, Kansas still would not be a free state because other parts of the constitution, not to be voted on under the Lecompton rules, guaranteed that slaves already in Kansas could be kept lawfully. Actually, the Lecompton constitutional convention had loaded the dice; and that is why the Free Soil supporters refused to go to the polls.

The new Kansas legislature met on December 7, just two weeks before the Lecompton vote was to be held. There was nothing the legislature could do to stop the voting, because it was called under Kansas law, but the legislature could call another election. The lawmakers did just that. The second election, they said, would show what people in Kansas really thought about the matter of slavery, because the people would vote on the whole constitution, not just one article. Did they want the Lecompton Constitution protecting slavery, or not? The decision would be reached January 4, 1858.

When President Buchanan learned that Secretary Stanton had convened the legislature, he became angry and removed Stanton from office. Governor Walker resigned. Senator Douglas quarreled with President Buchanan, harsh words were spoken, and the two broke off relations. Now, for the first time, the Democratic party itself faced an open split among its most important leaders.

On December 21, the Lecompton Constitution was ratified by a vote of 6,226 to 569. (Of the votes, 2,720 were later proved to be fraudulent.)

Less than three weeks later the second election was held.

On January 4, the people were called upon to decide on the whole constitution. The pro-slavery people, by and large, boycotted this election. The vote was 162 for the Lecompton Constitution and 10,226 against it.

Here in the two elections, discounting the fraudulent votes, could be seen the real state of public opinion in Kansas. Ten thousand voters wanted a free state, and four thousand wanted a slave state.

President Buchanan chose to ignore these figures and events. On January 30, 1858, the president of the Lecompton convention delivered the Lecompton Constitution to the White House, with the request that it be placed before Congress.

In planning his course, President Buchanan turned to the Supreme Court, which he respected so much, and took his course from a decision made by that court in 1857. The decision was called the Dred Scott decision.

The Dred Scott case began in 1834, when Dr. John Emerson, an army surgeon, moved from St. Louis, Missouri, to Rock Island, Illinois. He took his household with him, including a slave named Dred Scott. Legally, Rock Island was out of bounds for the slave because in 1787 Congress had ruled that there would be no slavery in Illinois. Actually, no one disturbed Dred Scott or his master in Rock Island.

Later, Dr. Emerson was transferred to Fort Snelling in Wisconsin Territory, and he took Dred Scott with him. Slavery was forbidden in the Wisconsin Territory by the Missouri Compromise, which outlawed slavery in all the Louisiana Purchase territory of the North and West.

In 1846 Dr. Emerson returned to St. Louis. There, Dred Scott sued for his freedom, saying that between 1834 and 1838 he had lived in territory where slavery was outlawed and therefore he was a free man.

The federal district court judge ruled in favor of Scott. The case was appealed by Scott's owner and finally reached the United States Supreme Court.

The majority of the members of the Supreme Court voted that the court had no jurisdiction in this case because Dred Scott was a slave and not a citizen of the United States. The Supreme Court usually decides whether or not it has jurisdiction in a case and, if not, refuses to comment any further on the law involved. But in the Dred Scott case, the court first decided it had no jurisdiction and then made many points about the slavery situation.

Most important was the point that although a slave might travel with his master through free states and territories where slavery was outlawed, this travel did not free the slave. Congress had no right to meddle with slavery, nor had anyone else, because the property right of slaves was recognized in the Fifth Amendment to the Constitution, which said that Congress could not deprive persons of property without due process of law.

On the basis of the Dred Scott decision, Buchanan reached his own decision on the Lecompton Constitution. He referred the Lecompton Constitution to Congress along with a message that listed the following points:

First, the Lecompton Constitution had been framed in a free and open balloting which the convention had ordered to be taken on the question of slavery.

Second, he said, the question of slavery in Kansas was thus confined to the people of Kansas.

Third, if Congress should now reject the Lecompton Constitution because it had slavery in it, the agitation on the matter of slavery would be renewed and intensified all over America.

Fourth, he realized that most of the people of Kansas did not want slavery, and he quite expected that the new

legislature would take action under the constitution to out-
law slavery. That was perfectly all right; it was the privilege
of the people to amend their constitution as they saw fit.

Fifth, President Buchanan said, if Congress refused to
accept the Lecompton Constitution because it sanctioned
slavery, a second constitution would have to be framed and
sent to Congress all over again, and then the struggle about
slavery would begin again, making more trouble throughout the nation than ever.

Sixth, he said, the speedy admission of Kansas would restore peace and harmony to the country, and this was much
more important than worrying about the small difference
of time it would take the people of Kansas to hold another
election and to modify their new constitution.

President Buchanan has often been accused of favoring
the slaveholders. From the above it is apparent that this
was not the case, nor was the President blind or too stub-
born to realize what was happening in Kansas. He was concerned about the entire nation, however, and about the
frightening attacks of temper that he saw around him.

Buchanan's position was exactly in accordance with his
character; he believed in the rule of law and the strict ad-
herence to legal forms. He quite expected the Free Soil
majority of Kansas to change the constitution. But in his
message to Congress he was issuing a call for greatness, the
greatness of abstinence, from men who were moved to
strong emotion by the subject of slavery.

This was Buchanan's great weakness, speaking from the
vantage point of history. It was not weakness of character,
but weakness of vision. Buchanan was willing to accept the
attacks from members of his own party led by Senator
Douglas. He was willing to countenance the resignation
of his appointed governor of Kansas and the ensuing de-
nunciations from the northern press. He stood firm in his

belief that the Kansas question could be settled in Kansas by Kansas and that this was the will of Congress and that it should thus be done.

There was an alternate course which Buchanan could have taken, and in taking it he might have achieved greatness. The Lecompton Constitution could have been rejected by the President because of fraudulent voting. The pattern was clear, and had been for several years—the southerners were stuffing the ballot boxes. But to have rejected the constitution because of fraud would have been to throw down the gauntlet to the South, accusing southerners of illegal tactics. Buchanan, seeing hope of a simple solution if men would only listen to reason instead of erupting in emotion, rejected this course.

Ruled as he was by intellect, it is hard to see how James Buchanan could have followed any other course than the one he chose. He did not realize that the slavery issue had burst the bounds of reason and that men who only a few years before could have been persuaded by intellectual argument were now living on their emotions.

Buchanan did not come easily to his decisions, nor was he simply overwhelmed by his cabinet. He sat down in the privacy of his study in the White House and agonized over the Kansas decision. In his own hand he wrote out a lengthy essay on the Kansas-Nebraska Act. He studied the Dred Scott decision again. He studied everything he could find, and still he came to the same conclusion.

So it was done, and the message was given to Congress. Congress reacted as he knew it would, with "a long, exciting, and occasionally violent debate in both houses" which lasted for three months.

He noted sadly that in the course of the debate "slavery was denounced in every form which could exasperate the southern people and render it odious to the people of the

North; whilst on the other hand many of the speeches of southern members displayed characteristic violence."

During the course of this debate, the breach with Senator Douglas became complete and irrevocable. Douglas spoke hotly against the President, and Buchanan retaliated by removing Douglas supporters from office and refusing to appoint supporters of Douglas and his friends to federal office. He levied the important patronage power against those of his own party who disagreed with him, and in doing this he split the Democratic party more widely than he knew.

As far as Kansas was concerned, events proved that if the nation could be pushed into obedience to law and intellect, the problem of slavery could be solved. After three months of congressional debate the Lecompton Constitution was accepted, but with an important amendment to the law: the Crittenden-Montgomery Amendment provided that the constitution be resubmitted to the voters of Kansas.

On August 2, 1858, the voters of Kansas went to the polls to express their opinions on the constitution for the third time. In the voting 11,812 people voted against accepting the constitution, and 1,926 voted in favor of it. So here again was proof that the vast majority of Kansas wanted a free state.

By rejecting the constitution, Kansas voters decided that they would remain in territorial status. And once the political issue was quieted, all the trouble in Kansas evaporated. John Brown, the Connecticut abolitionist, went elsewhere to stir emotions. The private armies of the southerners and the Free Soil men disappeared, and Kansas settled down to a normal life, in which a handful of slaveowners lived peaceably among their non-slave-holding brothers. For the most part, slaveholders left Kansas, taking their slaves with them. Events in Kansas proved that, in principle, James Buchanan was exactly right.

Yet there is more to politics than principle, and it was as a politician, exercising the arts of government, that James Buchanan failed in the Kansas crisis. Senator Douglas led a group called "the Northern Democracy" which virtually moved outside the Democratic party after the issue of the Lecompton Constitution was raised. The remainder, largely southerners, began to call themselves "the Old Democracy," and reaffirmed their belief in the sanctity of the right of property—which meant slavery.

The issue that was to bring about civil war was exposed fully in that spring of 1858, and it was apparent that there was no going back and that the unity of the Democratic party was in shreds.

Less than a year after the beginning of his administration, the power James Buchanan had hoped to wield to keep the Union together was lying in tatters. His party was splintered, and the northern wing held him in the utmost contempt as a traitor to his own state and to the cause of freedom. The southerners, who supported Buchanan in his position on the Lecompton Constitution, did not do so for Buchanan's lofty motives but for the preservation of slavery. Consequently, the battle won, and yet lost, the southerners had little use for the man who had taken a position that seemed to be theirs. They sensed, although the northerners did not, that Buchanan was no friend of slavery, and they distrusted him as much as the northern Democrats did.

James Buchanan, then, was isolated from both branches of the Democratic party. Southerners in Congress were already talking about what they would demand at the next Democratic national convention when it came time to select a candidate and fix a platform. They would demand an outright endorsement of slavery in the platform or a candidate from the South who would, of course, stand straight for slavery in every way. This meant that in 1858 the Democrats of the South had already cast James Buchanan aside as a possible candidate to succeed himself. Buchanan was aware of this, and he knew there was no chance that he might achieve support from the North, for even if Stephen A. Douglas relented in his own ambition, the enmity on the issue of Kansas could not be dissipated.

President Buchanan's political fortunes were destroyed, but not his position as President and statesman. He could not function successfully as a leader of the nation in domestic affairs, but he could and did function successfully as leader of the nation in matters that affected American relationships with other countries.

Buchanan was admirably suited to be his own Secretary of State, for he had long years of service as a diplomat behind him. Lewis Cass of Michigan was Secretary of State in the Buchanan cabinet, but Cass was not a diplomat, either by nature or by training, and it fell upon the President to prepare the groundwork for most of the decisions, as well as to make the decisions themselves.

Two issues in the realm of foreign affairs troubled the nation when James Buchanan came to the Presidency. Both concerned the uneasy relations of the United States with England. One was the problem of the British protectorate over the Mosquito Coast, which Buchanan had faced before and which he settled with new treaties under which the British ceased, finally, their attempts to create new colonies in the Americas. The second was the problem of search and seizure of American ships. This British practice had brought about the War of 1812. Late in the 1850's it again threatened relations between the two countries, because the British were making a serious effort to stamp out the African slave trade and they infringed on American rights.

In 1842 the British and American governments had each agreed to keep a squadron of ships off the coast of Africa to stop their citizens from trading in slaves. English ships took the position that they could stop and search any merchant vessel which appeared suspicious to them. The British government extended this practice to the waters of the new world and sent a number of ships to the Gulf of Mexico and the Caribbean where they stopped all suspected merchant ships. The South was indignant, but so were the shipowners of New England and the central states. This was one matter on which North and South could still agree. President Buchanan sent an American squadron to the neighborhood of Cuba with orders to protect all American ships from detention by foreign warships and not to avoid aggressive action if it became necessary. The British quickly withdrew from the area.

There was trouble with Mexico during the Buchanan administration. The nation to the south seemed beset with revolution. President Cononfort was elected in the fall of 1857, but he was driven from Mexico City a month after he took office. Then, one general followed another to power: Juarez, Zuloaga, and Miramon. American citizens were arrested and shot without trial. American property was seized, and American claims against Mexico were ignored. President Buchanan asked Congress in his annual message of 1859 to authorize the dispatch of a force to Mexico to preserve American lives and to assert American claims if that became necessary. Congress was too busy worrying about slavery. Again, in 1860, Buchanan repeated the request, and again Congress ignored him. Thus, in the intolerable confusion that persisted in Mexico, it was sim-

ple for the French to move in when war troubled the
United States a few months later, and Louis Napoleon in
Paris decided to establish a new colony in Mexico. Maxi-
milian, a prince of the house of Hapsburg, was dispatched
to the new world as Emperor of Mexico three years later,
after an invasion of Vera Cruz conducted in concert with
Britain and Spain.

There was trouble with Paraguay. Following the traditional policy of strength, which was part of the American
attitude toward the western hemisphere, the American
steamer "Water Witch" was dispatched under a naval commander to survey various rivers in South America and to
determine their navigability. Paraguay's President Lopez
took exception to American ships steaming up the Parana
River, and a Paraguayan soldier fired on the steamer and
killed the helmsman.

A naval force of nineteen ships carrying 2,500 sailors
and Marines was dispatched to South America and, backed
by the force, an American commissioner was able to secure
redress. In his annual message of 1859, Buchanan announced with satisfaction that there was no further trouble
with Paraguay. She had, indeed, been coerced into treaties
and into submission.

CHAPTER 9

The Eve of War

FOLLOWING THE DECISION on the Lecompton Constitution and the open breach with Senator Douglas, President Buchanan became the object of a malignant campaign to discredit him as a public official and even as a person. As with so many other public officials, the feeling that he had been either corrupt or weak persisted long after his death and after the issues were quieted by the peaceful intervention of time.

James Buchanan was every inch the gentleman and honest official. He maintained particularly friendly relations with Queen Victoria of England and Prince Albert, and when the Prince of Wales (Edward VII) visited Canada Buchanan invited him to come to the United States as well. The Prince came in October, 1860, and enjoyed himself immensely. Buchanan and his niece, Harriet Lane, who was also his official hostess at the White House, took the royal party on a steamer trip to see Mount Vernon. It was a gay affair with champagne and liquors and delicate foods. When it was over, and the Secretary of the Treasury proposed to pay the bill out of public funds, President Buchanan insisted that it be paid privately. However, since it had been the Secretary's idea to spend so much money, the treasury paid the bill.

It seemed only fair. On his salary of $25,000 a year, President Buchanan found it difficult to refrain from digging deep into his own resources to maintain the White House. During the winter months he held state dinners once a week in the large dining room which seated forty persons. Once each week he invited the cabinet members and their wives to dinner, and always, it seemed, there were some outsiders at his table.

He worked hard in his office on the southwest side of the second story of the White House, from eight o'clock in the morning until luncheon at one. After lunch he went back to the office to work until five, when he usually took a walk around Washington, talking to people. He seldom drove out in the coach unless it was summer; then he commuted to the White House from a stone cottage in the hills near Washington called the Soldier's Home.

Buchanan was careful about financial matters and his use of the public trust. He was much opposed to nepotism and would not appoint those close to him to permanent positions. His nephew, for example, was his private secretary, and when the administration was drawing to a close, he wistfully hoped that he might obtain a job as a paymaster in the navy because he wanted to travel and see the world. The nephew was afraid to ask Buchanan to appoint him. Then a judge whom the President had appointed suggested that the young man become his clerk. J. Buchanan Henry asked his uncle about the idea, and was informed that it would not be seemly or good public policy. Buchanan would accept no gifts for himself or for his household. He was strong-willed and austere in his personal habits. When Harriet Lane went to New York to buy furniture for the rundown White House, he wrote and warned her that there was only $8,000 left in an appropriation made by Congress for the purpose and that if she spent more he would have to pay for it himself. Another time, when his niece unwisely used the White House yacht "Harriet Lane" for a trip to West Point and the newspapers complained, Buchanan wrote chiding her:

> I am sorry to find that your excursion to West Point on the "Harriet Lane" has been made the subject of newspaper criticism of yourself. This is most ungallant and ungentlemanly. The practice, however, of employing national vessels on pleasure excursions, to gratify any class of people, is a fair subject of public criticism. You know how much I condemned your former trip on the same vessel, and I did not expect you would fall into a second error. The thing, however, is past and gone, and let it pass. After a fair time shall have elapsed, it is my purpose to cause general orders to be issued by the Treasury and Naval Departments to put a stop to the practice.

That short note indicated another aspect of James Buchanan's character. Having chided his niece for her conduct, the matter was forgotten, for the President bore few grudges, and he was always ready to make up with his enemies—except for a few, who continued to attack him. Some saw weakness in this geniality, and for years after his administration he was called a weak man.

The personal campaign of defamation against James Buchanan grew more heated in the autumn of 1859 and in early 1860. The tone was established in Congress, where hatred of Buchanan grew in the minds of the northerners.

In the spring of 1860, the House of Representatives was under the control of a coalition of Whigs, the new Republicans, and northern Democrats who could agree on at least one point: their hatred of James Buchanan. On March 5, 1860, Representative Covode of Pennsylvania introduced a resolution calling for an investigation of the President's conduct, with a very definite plan to try to impeach him. (It is interesting that Representative Covode was also the

man who introduced the resolution to impeach President
Andrew Johnson eight years later.)

The resolution called for the appointment of a committee of five members of the House, who would conduct a
secret investigation of President Buchanan's actions. The
investigation began early in March.

Nothing quite like this had ever before occurred in
American politics. Reading about it in the newspapers, the
people tended to believe that where there was smoke there
might be fire, and President Buchanan's reputation declined further. He fought back vigorously, however. On
March 28, he transmitted a strong protest to the House of
Representatives against the indignity of a secret investigation of his official acts. The Covode resolution had hinted
that Buchanan had tried to use patronage, money, and improper influence to secure passage of certain laws and that
he had failed to execute the laws of the land. Buchanan
charged that this was a political investigation, called to embarrass him, and that it was disgraceful for the House of
Representatives to be so used.

The investigation continued until the middle of June.
The President's protest was rejected by the House on
strictly party lines. In June, however, after all the innu-
endos and partial testimony were revealed, to try to show
that the President had misbehaved, the House could not
find any real evidence of such misbehavior, and the investigation was dropped. On June 28, President Buchanan sent
another message to the House, accusing its members of making "false and atrocious" charges, and of playing filthy
politics without regard for the good of the nation. He urged
the House to stop making wild charges for the benefit of
the press and, if there was a case, to begin to make it.

This communication was referred to a select committee
of the House, with orders to report at the session scheduled

for December. By common consent the matter was allowed
to die. The election came between; James Buchanan had
refused to be a candidate although some Democrats wanted
him. (Not very many Democrats wanted Buchanan in the
spring and summer of 1860, and he knew it. The South
demanded a southern candidate or a slavery plank, and
the North was committed to Stephen Douglas.) In December, 1860, even Buchanan's enemies had other things to
think about because it was apparent that unless a miracle
occurred the Union was to be dissolved.

By April, after the Covode Investigation had begun,
James Buchanan had decided flatly that his name was not
going to be bandied about at the Charleston convention of
the Democratic party that summer. He had indicated as
much in his inaugural address and when he accepted the
nomination in 1856, but in the Presidency men often
change their minds. Buchanan did not. In his inaugural
address he said, "Having determined not to become a candidate for reelection, I shall have no motive to influence my
conduct in administering the government except the desire
ably and faithfully to serve my country, and to live in the
grateful memory of my countrymen."

By April, 1860, James Buchanan knew that if he ever
achieved the "grateful memory" of his countrymen it
would not be during his lifetime. Seldom had a President
been subjected to such calumny even though he was not
seeking public office again. Men in the North—Whigs, Republicans, the followers of John Bell, and northern Democrats—blamed Buchanan for all the ills of the nation. The
southerners accused him of not supporting their cause as
they had expected him to do.

In the campaign that followed, Buchanan could not support Douglas, who had proved so inimical to him in both
political and personal affairs. He supported James Breck-

inridge, the candidate of the southern Democrats, but he told his friends they must make up their own minds in good conscience as to their own courses. In a speech from the White House portico on July 9, he noted that the Charleston convention had failed to nominate a Democratic candidate and that neither the convention which nominated Douglas nor that which nominated Breckinridge could be called a convention of the whole Democratic party. Every Democrat should vote as he saw fit, Buchanan said. Personally, he believed the property rights of southerners must be protected and he would vote for Breckinridge. Again, Buchanan had reduced the moral issue of slavery to its simplest legal component, losing the moral problem in the process. Slaves were property, he said. The Supreme Court had so ruled in the Dred Scott case, and there was nothing more to say.

James Buchanan proved himself a bad prophet as he made this speech in the summer of 1860.

> There is but one possible contingency which can endanger the Union, and against this all Democrats, whether squatter sovereigns or popular sovereigns, will present a united resistance. Should the time ever arrive when northern agitation and fanaticism shall proceed so far as to render the domestic firesides of the South insecure, then, and not till then, will the Union be in danger. A United Northern Democracy will present a wall of fire against such a catastrophe.

Even on the eve of the election, James Buchanan honestly believed that the agitation against slavery was prompted by northern abolitionists and that it was producing nothing but mischief in America. He hoped that slavery could gradually be abolished by people within the various states, but he would not accept the idea that there was a "higher law" than the Constitution of the United

States, or that slavery could be abolished without the consent of the slaveowners themselves.

Except for that one speech, President Buchanan took no part in the election of 1860. He let his views be known to friends and others in correspondence, and they were used by both his friends and his enemies. The President, however, was ready to retire from active politics after forty years.

On the eve of the election, General Winfield Scott, often a candidate for the Presidency himself, and chief of staff of the army at that time, wrote the President that he feared if Lincoln were elected there would be a move in the South to secede and that the nine southern federal forts ought to be strengthened with larger garrisons to prevent their capture and civil war. Buchanan ignored these views. Scott apparently could never do anything quietly. Had he come to the President privately, he might have been heard. He chose, instead, to make his views known in a letter, which he had copied and distributed to his friends. He was apparently not nearly so interested in what he had to say as that it be made public. Buchanan took the position that to strengthen the forts in the South on the eve of the election would be to announce a policy of force and to frighten the southerners into the belief that their future was indeed in danger.

Aided by the knowledge of history one can say that Scott's view was reasonable and that President Buchanan's view was not. And yet, here we have the basic differences between types of men: Scott was a soldier, and soldiers are always planning for action without regard to the political consequences. Politics is the responsibility of the politicians, they say, and it is proper that this should be so. Soldiers, however, usually make their war plans secretly, and not for public consumption. Buchanan was a conciliator, a diplomat, a politician. He saw the crisis not in terms of black and white, but in terms of the wrongs and excesses of both sides, and he hoped to buy time to bring about conciliation.

Had the President ordered all the available standing armies into the nine southern forts, it is most doubtful that this action would have affected the basic decisions of the southern leaders. Perhaps it might have affected them: it might have brought about the secession even more quickly and might have caused even more lives to have been lost than were spent in the opening days of the war.

Buchanan took the position that as President of all the United States he could not assume that part of the Union was planning to secede. His responsibility, as long as he remained in office, was to all the people, for he was their representative. Speaking from the point of view of law, this was a sound argument.

General Scott's views were still under consideration by his friends when the election was held and Abraham Lincoln was chosen as the new President. Immediately, the legislature of South Carolina assembled and called for a convention of the people of that state on December 17, 1860.

South Carolina was the logical place for the dissatisfaction to erupt. South Carolina was the home of John C. Calhoun, the father of the doctrine of "nullification," which held that any state had the right to go its own way when it did not approve of the Union course. Calhoun was dead, but his ideas lived on.

In the weeks following the national election, the people of South Carolina selected delegates to the convention of December 17, and when it met it took them just three days to decide that they would secede from the Union. They did this by voting to repeal the Ordinance of 1788, by which the state had ratified the Constitution of the United States. Their position was that they had joined the Union voluntarily and that they were now choosing to go out of it because its direction threatened the basic rights of the people of South Carolina.

Taking the view of the followers of Calhoun, that position was perfectly understandable. The people of South Carolina did not believe that they had irrevocably cast their lot with the union of states back in 1788. They believed that state government was the basic unit of government and that the federal union existed only to serve the joint purposes of the states. If the states found themselves in disagreement with one another, following this theory, there was nothing to prevent them from dissolving the old union and forming such new union as they wished with states of like mind.

Troubled by this decision, President Buchanan wrote his Attorney-General, Jeremiah Black of Pennsylvania, asking what he was legally bound to do in case of conflict between state and federal authorities. Black replied that the power to decide what action might be taken against an offending state rested in Congress and that the President could not order troops into any state or wage war against any state.

Thus, in his annual message to Congress of December, 1860, President Buchanan was faced with the problem of certain secession. The secession had not actually begun when the President prepared his message, but the course of South Carolina was clear. Buchanan lamented the "long, continued, and intemperate interference of the northern people with the question of slavery in the southern states," but said it was not yet too late to stop the crisis. All that was necessary, he said, was for the states to leave each other alone and for each state to solve its own problems relative to slavery. "As sovereign states," he said, "they and they alone are responsible before God and the world for the slavery existing among them."

It appeared that President Buchanan was taking the side of the South. But that was not the case; he also said that the southern states had absolutely no right to secede and could not secede. As to the Union, he said, "It was intended to be perpetual, and not to be annulled at the pleasure of any one of the contracting parties."

At that point, however, the President's logic broke. The Union was to be perpetual and secession was illegal, but neither the chief executive nor Congress could authorize the federal forces to take action to prevent states from seceding. The President went so far with his logic, and then abandoned it in the hope—now useless—that war could be averted. The states had no right to secede, he said, but the people of the states had the inherent right, above all constitutions, to engage in revolution against the established government if it became intolerable to them. This statement went back further than the Constitution of the United States to the Declaration of Independence of the thirteen colonies.

The right of revolution is inherent in America, for the United States was founded in revolution; but while Americans as a people may accept the right of revolution, the United States as a government may not. While James Buchanan as an individual could accept and understand the conditions under which certain Americans would rebel against the Union, President Buchanan had no lawful right to discuss revolution. The government of the United States was a legal entity, which had every responsibility to protect itself and to attempt to put down revolution. When James Buchanan became President of the United States, he abnegated his desires and responsibilities as a simple citizen and became chief executive of the government. In discussing the conditions under which revolution might come, he was not living up to his obligations to the United States, but was tacitly giving encouragement to revolution and the southern secessionists.

The presidential message pleased neither North nor South. The North objected because the President temporized; the South objected because the President indicated that even if the states seceded he would seek to enforce the laws of the United States, which would mean the maintenance of forts in the South, the collection of customs by the United States government at southern ports, and the continued conduct of other federal business in the southern states.

Senator Jefferson Davis of Mississippi arose in Congress and denounced President Buchanan's message. Northern senators also denounced the message as giving aid to the South. Of all in the Senate, perhaps only Andrew Johnson of Tennessee saw the point that President Buchanan was trying to make. Johnson, a strict Constitutionalist himself, put it this way:

I do not believe the federal government has the power to coerce a state, for by the Eleventh Amendment of the Constitution of the United States it is expressly provided that you cannot even put one of the states of this confederacy before one of the court of the country as a party (in a suit). As a state, the federal government has no power to coerce it, but it as a member of the compact to which it agreed in common with the other states, and this government has the right to pass laws and to enforce those laws upon individuals within the limits of each state. While the one proposition is clear, the other is equally so. This government can, by the Constitution of the country, and by the laws enacted in conformity with the Constitution, operate upon individuals, and has the right and the power, not to coerce a state,

but to enforce and execute the law upon individuals within the limits
of a state.

There were very few people in America who could see
above the heat of their emotions that the President was
right. Nor, in view of his involved message to Congress, did
the southerners believe that Buchanan intended to maintain federal troops in the South in order to force southerners to obey the federal laws whether their states seceded
or not.

In December, President Buchanan sent Caleb Cushing
to Charleston as his personal representative, hoping to persuade Governor Pickens against the course of secession.
But, on December 20, the secession ordinance was passed
without a dissenting vote, and two days later three South
Carolina citizens were appointed to go to Washington to
treat with the government regarding the new relationship
between South Carolina and the United States. Major Anderson, the commander of the federal garrison in Charleston, dismantled Fort Moultrie, spiked the fort's guns, and
moved his command to Fort Sumter, located on an island in
the harbor. He took this action to show the people of
Charleston that he intended to defend federal property and
to remain in the heart of what might be enemy country.

On December 28 President Buchanan met with the commissioners from South Carolina. He warned them, on introduction, that he was seeing them as private parties, not
as representatives of the sovereign state of South Carolina.
They insisted that Major Anderson would have to evacuate
Fort Sumter before there could be any discussion.

Then, on December 31, President Buchanan learned that
the South Carolina authorities had seized Fort Moultrie,
the post office, and the customs office and that every federal
official in Charleston had resigned his post. The authorities

had captured Major Humphreys, the officer in charge of the arsenal, and had seized a half million dollars' worth of arms. Fort Sumter was the only piece of Union property in Charleston still in Union hands.

President Buchanan rejected the demand of the South Carolina commissioners for withdrawal of the troops and warned them that Fort Sumter would be defended.

In December, Lewis Cass resigned as Secretary of State because he disagreed with the President on the question of reinforcing the federal garrison at Charleston. Cass believed that the garrison ought to be strengthened and that the customs house ought to be moved to Fort Sumter, thus making it possible for the federal authorities to collect duty on incoming shipments of goods. Buchanan would not take these steps because he felt they would only provoke South Carolina to stronger action and because he still hoped for reconciliation.

A few days later, President Buchanan decided to send reinforcements aboard the steamer "Brooklyn" to Fort Sumter, whereupon Secretary of the Interior Jacob Thompson of Mississippi resigned. Then Philip Thomas of Maryland, who had been Secretary of the Treasury for less than a month, resigned. John B. Floyd, the Secretary of War, also resigned. Buchanan said this resignation was demanded after he discovered that Floyd was involved in the theft of $870,000 in bonds held in trust for various Indian tribes; Floyd said he resigned because he could not countenance the invasion of the South by reinforcements to the Charleston garrison.

Attempts were made in Congress, in December and January, to compromise the differences between the states. Senator Crittenden of Kentucky suggested that a line be drawn at 36° 30', above which slavery would be excluded. Below that line, southerners could take slaves into the territories, but when the states were established they should be admitted as free or slave states, according to the wishes of the people. The compromise failed, in spite of having received the support of the President. Neither North nor South were listening now. The South was arming and making ready to walk out of the Union, and the North waited, standing on principle, but not really believing what the eyes of men everywhere saw—that there was going to be a war.

The steamer "Star of the West" moved to Charleston harbor to discharge troops, but she was fired on by the South Carolinians, and she withdrew. South Carolina sent another emissary to Washington, proposing that South Carolina buy Fort Sumter from the federal government, but Buchanan refused.

By February 4, six of the southern states had seceded from the Union. Now, all President James Buchanan could do was conduct a holding action for another month, waiting until March 4 when Abraham Lincoln would take office and the terrible responsibility for the affairs of the nation.

Buchanan could do virtually nothing under his interpretation of his powers. He felt that Congress must act to give him power, but Congress refused or was unable to act. Buchanan wrote:

We have already seen that Congress, throughout the entire session, refused to adopt any measures of compromise to prevent civil war or to retain first the cotton or afterward the border states within the Union. Failing to do this, and whilst witnessing the secession of one after another of the cotton states, the withdrawal of their senators and representatives, and the formation of their Confederacy, it was the imperative duty of Congress to furnish the President or his successor the means of repelling force by force, should this become necessary to preserve the Union. They, nevertheless, refused to perform this duty, with as much pertinacity as they had manifested in repudiating all measures of compromise.

So the Buchanan administration drew to an end in February, paralyzed by inactivity. Within the cabinet there were rumors that an attempt would be made to seize Washington and the Capitol, and turn them over to the Confederates. The President warned Congress that some of his officials shared this fear. Congress investigated, but discovered no plot.

The days dragged on, Buchanan doing his best to maintain a level state of public affairs so that he could turn the government over to Abraham Lincoln without the charge that he had precipitated war. Under the circumstances, that was his idea of the best he could do for the nation.

On March 4, the fateful day arrived, and James Buchanan and Abraham Lincoln shared a carriage which drove up Pennsylvania Avenue to the Capitol for the inauguration. There were no political discussions between incoming and retiring Presidents; there was no meeting of the minds. Lincoln did not request any information. And on March 9, 1861, James Buchanan returned to his estate at Wheatland, a private citizen, to watch and wait with the rest of the nation.

CHAPTER 10

Last Days

JAMES BUCHANAN at least left Washington in the company of his friends; his neighbors in Lancaster County had sent a delegation to Washington to escort the retiring President home. A military escort took him to the Washington Railroad station, where he entrained for Baltimore. At Barnum's Hotel in Baltimore he stopped to make a speech and to receive a serenade from supporters in Maryland.

Baltimore city guards escorted him to York and other points in Pennsylvania, and at Lancaster he was greeted by a committee of around 150 people and was taken to a meeting of citizens who had assembled from several of the surrounding counties. He spoke, expressing his hope that God would preserve the Union and the Constitution, and then he sat down in his carriage and was driven west toward Wheatland.

He was scarcely home before the war began, with the firing of the South Carolina batteries on Fort Sumter early in the morning of April 12, 1861. There was nothing more to be done. The struggle must be fought unto the end.

Buchanan remained in Lancaster during the war years, gathering his papers and attempting to clarify the positions he had taken during the last months before the beginning of war.

He was forced to protect himself against demeaning remarks. Newspaper articles accused him of having taken from the White House articles intended as gifts from Queen Victoria and others to the chief of state, which meant they belonged to the inmate of the White House and not to any other person. It was true that Queen Victoria had sent some pictures to Miss Lane, and his niece took them with her, but they had been sent as a personal gift. And as for other items, particularly some Japanese rarities that Buchanan was virtually accused of stealing, he had had those delivered to the patent office for safekeeping long before he left the White House.

In correspondence with his old cabinet members and others, Buchanan followed the policies of the new administration and the conduct of the war. When it began, he wrote sadly to his nephew that "the confederate states have deliberately commenced the civil war, and God knows where it may end. They were repeatedly warned by my administration that an assault on Fort Sumter would be civil war, and they would be responsible for the consequences."

However, Buchanan favored the war, once begun. "The North will sustain the administration almost to a man," he wrote to a friend, "and it ought to be sustained at all hazards."

Buchanan fell ill in the spring of 1861, but he recovered and settled down to work on his papers. He heard encouraging words about the future of the Democratic party for 1864, but he did not believe them, and when General McClellan was defeated by Lincoln in that election he was not in the least surprised. In the autumn of 1864 he hoped for a conciliation with the Confederacy, but he did not really expect the administration to bring it about. He consoled himself with the thought that he had been the guardian of the Constitution, no matter what else had happened during his administration.

In the spring of 1865, when President Lincoln was assassinated, the word came quickly to Wheatland. Buchanan deplored the terrible act. "I deeply mourn his loss," he said, "from private feelings, but still more deeply for the sake of the country. Heaven, I trust, will not suffer the perpetrators of the deed and all their guilty accomplices to escape just punishment."

He had faith in Andrew Johnson, the new President, however, because he recognized in Johnson a fellow Constitutionalist who had, to Buchanan's mind, sound judgment and excellent common sense. He began to have his doubts about Johnson in the summer, but held his tongue except with friends.

Buchanan's niece, Harriet Lane, married a Baltimore man named Johnston, and the former President was left more alone in the house outside Lancaster. He became involved in local charities and local affairs, and, in 1866 and 1867, these matters and his health occupied most of his attention. He prepared a defense of his administration for publication, but when Horace Greeley, the Republican editor, asked him for material in his own defense, he refused to submit it. He suffered sometimes from gout and from intestinal disorders.

Buchanan kept up his interest in Democratic politics, and when the reconstruction acts began to come along he advised his Democratic friends to remain true to the principle of states' rights and to oppose Negro suffrage on a national basis because it was the business of the states to regulate voting in their own territories.

He suffered a bad fall in the autumn of 1867 going down the porch steps of his house, and perhaps he did not ever quite recover from it. At seventy-seven he had begun to feel that he was very old. The illness on his return from Washington had made him weak, and he seemed to feel that with that return his productive life was over, and he was only awaiting death.

In the spring of 1878 James Buchanan fell ill again while on a visit to Cape May. He was brought home an invalid, and this time he was certain that he was going to die. He asked for his brother, the Rev. George Buchanan, who came to the household but returned to his own home near Philadelphia a few days later when James seemed to be improving. On June 1, however, James Buchanan died, having spent his last few hours quite lucid and free from suffering, selecting his burial place and putting his affairs finally in order. On June 4, he was buried after a simple ceremony in Lancaster.

During those last years in seclusion, James Buchanan had no fear and no regrets for the manner in which he had conducted himself in the Presidency. He told a friend one day that he believed posterity would do him justice, that he had done all he could to save the Union and that history would vindicate his memory.

In fact, history had not vindicated his memory a century later, for even after the millions of words written to explain the Civil War and its causes and the thousands of books published on every aspect of the war, Americans found it difficult to understand the reasoning of men caught up in the events and emotions of those times. Slavery was not the issue alone, nor economics, nor the feeling that the South was somehow being swallowed by the behemoth of the industrial North. There was a strong feeling, which had existed since the earliest days of the Republic, for the states and their rights. In the massive migrations across the nation at the end of the Civil War, much of the state feeling was lost, but, until the 1850's, many men considered themselves first citizens of their states and then citizens of the United States, and they would no more think of moving permanently outside the state of their birth than they would think of going to live in a foreign land.

History has been unkind to James Buchanan, not because he acted so much more wisely than historians now believe, not because he rose to greatness, for he did not, but because he is so often judged by yardsticks foreign to his times. He was a religious man in a way, and he detested slavery personally, but he never took it upon himself to make moral judgments of the conduct of his fellow men in this regard. As he said, slavery was the moral problem of the people of the South, and he divested himself of responsibility for it.

Greatness would have demanded that he somehow overcome the problem, cause the downfall of slavery, and hold the Union together in spite of it. He had no such greatness in his soul, nor perhaps had any other man of his day.

James Buchanan's body lies quietly in its grave in Lancaster, Pennsylvania. His epitaph might be: If men a century after his death could not understand or resolve the problems he faced, how could he be blamed for failure?

BIBLIOGRAPHY

AUCHAMPAUGH, PHILIP. *James Buchanan the Squire from Lancaster.* Undated pamphlet.

BUCHANAN, JAMES. *The Life of the Hon. James Buchanan (as written by himself and set to music by an old Democrat).* Political pamphlet, 1856.

CALDWELL, ROBERT GRANVILLE. *A Short History of the American People.* New York: G. P. Putnam's Sons, 1925.

CURTIS, GEORGE TICKNOR. *The Life of James Buchanan.* 2 vols. New York: Harper and Bros., 1883.

DEMOCRATIC STATE COMMITTEE OF PENNSYLVANIA. *Memoir of James Buchanan of Pennsylvania.* 1856.

HORTON, R. G. *The Life and Public Services of James Buchanan.* New York: Derby and Jackson, 1856.

JEROME, C. *Life of James Buchanan.* Claremont, N.H.: Tracy Kenney and Co., 1861.

KING, HORATIO. *Turning on the Light, a Dispassionate Survey of President Buchanan's Administration From 1860 to Its Close.* Philadelphia: J. B. Lippincott Company, 1895.

MINOR, HENRY. *The Story of the Democratic Party.* New York: The Macmillan Company, 1928.

MORRIS, RICHARD B. *Encyclopedia of American History.* New York: Harper and Bros., 1953.

INDEX